SOCIOLOGY AND
POLITICAL THEORY

SOCIOLOGY AND POLITICAL THEORY

A Consideration of the Sociological Basis of Politics

HARRY ELMER BARNES Ph. D.

Professor of Historical Sociology, Smith College

NEW YORK

ALFRED · A · KNOPF

MCMXXIV

HM
33
.B3

To

WILLIAM ARCHIBALD DUNNING

and

FRANKLIN HENRY GIDDINGS

CONTENTS

PREFACE

In 1915 the writer, at the suggestion of Professors William A. Dunning and Franklin H. Giddings of Columbia University, undertook the task of investigating the contributions of sociology to modern political theory, as the subject for a proposed doctoral dissertation. The work was largely completed before the end of 1917, but the cost of publication delayed its appearance. In the meantime, another enterprise was undertaken and utilized for the doctoral dissertation. Through the kindness and sympathetic coöperation of a number of editors of professional periodicals, especially those of the *American Journal of Sociology* and the English *Sociological Review,* it was possible to publish in the form of separate articles nearly all of the original study. During the period of their publication Professor Dunning suggested to the writer that he might well condense and reorganize this work, which was devoted to a survey of the opinions of individual sociologists, in such a way as to allow of a topical treatment and to secure a brief and succinct statement of the leading types of sociological contributions to the more important problems of political theory and the science of government. The present work represents an endeavor to execute this project.

To avoid any possible misunderstanding of the purpose of this book, it should be remarked at the outset that no attempt has been made to set forth an original and coherent sociological theory of the state. The sole aim is to introduce the reader to the more significant and representative types of sociological doctrines relating to the major problems of political science, and, by ample footnote references, to indicate how any suggestive interpretation may be more completely investigated. The adequacy and significance of the work must be held to depend solely upon the degree to which the author has succeeded in effecting an ingenious organization and an accurate exposition of the many and diverse sociological doctrines bearing on the topics selected. That wide differences of opinion exist among sociologists on almost every significant question is to be expected. In this respect they do not differ from historians, economists, political scientists, and students of ethics and philosophy. At the same time, there are usually stimulating interpretations offered from the most diverse points of view. The author does not in any way assume that the sociologists possess a monopoly of wisdom or insight with respect to political doctrine, but he does believe that the sociologists in the last half-century have made extremely significant contributions to every phase of political theory, and that no conscientious political scientist can well afford to remain ignorant of the nature and sources of such contributions. While the work is intended primarily as an introduction to the literature of the sociological theories of government and the state, it will also serve as a brief survey of sociological thought, interpreted from a topical rather than a personal point of view.

The writer desires at this time to express his gratitude to the many students of sociology and political science who have given him encouragement and assistance in carrying out his studies of social and political theory. Among such he would include, in particular, Franklin H. Giddings and William A. Dunning of Columbia University; Albion W. Small and Charles E. Merriam of the University of Chicago; Arthur N. Holcombe and William E. Hocking of Harvard University; Charles A. Beard and Alexander A. Goldenweiser of the New School for Social Research; Edgar Dawson of Hunter College; Charles A. Ellwood of the University of Missouri; Raymond G. Gettell of the University of California; and Ludwig Stein of the University of Berlin. Yet there is scarcely a sociologist of prominence in this country who has not, in one way or another, given evidence of a cordial interest in the subject under investigation, and rendered willing assistance whenever called upon. It is a matter of special satisfaction to the writer that his studies in this field, in both the personal and the topical arrangement, were completed before the lamented death of Professor Dunning and were thus able to profit by his kindly but acute criticism. I could not well conclude my inadequate summary of professional and academic indebtedness without mentioning the names of two men who have done far more than any others to shape my historical orientation and arouse my interest in the history of thought—James Thomson Shotwell and James Harvey Robinson.

H. E. B.

SOCIOLOGY AND
POLITICAL THEORY

CHAPTER I

THE DEVELOPMENT OF A SOCIOLOGICAL ORIENTATION IN POLITICAL THEORY

No better proof of the importance of sociological conceptions for political science can be brought forward than that afforded by briefly summarizing the prevailing views on the chief problems of political science and noting the fundamentally sociological bases and implications.[1] The state is no longer regarded as "a single unique entity existing alone in a circumambient void," to use Cole's phrase,[2] nor in Hegelian terminology as "perfected rationality," "the eternal and necessary essence of spirit," "the rational in itself and for itself," or the "absolute fixed end in itself"; but rather as a constituent society, or purposive association, akin to the many other functional organizations in modern society.[3] According to many recent writers on political theory, it is even doubtful whether

[1] Brief surveys of the nature and development of sociology, which will supplement this book in a helpful manner and aid in orienting the reader not at home in sociological literature, will be found in *American Journal of Sociology,* Vol. X, pp. 146 ff.; Vol. XXIII, pp. 174 ff. Cf. also Giddings, *Sociology: a Lecture;* Ross, *Foundations of Sociology,* pp. 256–352; Small, "Sociology," in *Encyclopedia Americana;* Tenney, "Some Recent Advances in Sociology," in *Political Science Quarterly,* Vol. XXV, pp. 500–22.

[2] *Social Theory,* p. 81.

[3] Cf. Duguit, *Law in the Modern State;* Follett, *The New State;* MacIver, *Community: a Sociological Study.*

1

the state can legitimately be differentiated from other organizations as being the only one possessed of the power
of using coercive force.[4]   By a majority it is now looked
upon chiefly as an umpire enforcing that minimum of
constraint which is essential to a peaceful and law-abiding
contention of the various "interest-groups" within society
—applying, as it were, the rules of the game which
govern the conflict of social groups and classes.[5]   By
an aggressive minority it is viewed primarily as the guardian of the rights of citizens as consumers, while the full
control of society in its productive capacity is to be
handed over to other functional organizations.[6]   Even
the vigorous advocates of state activity admit that, though
the state is a powerful instrument for promoting social
welfare and progress, it can be such only in so far as it
rests on sociological laws and an adequate knowledge of
the social forces involved.[7]   Further, the state is no longer
regarded as something which has existed from the beginning of history; rather it is generally understood that more
than nine-tenths of human history passed before the state
was evolved.   Hence, one must turn to human nature,
shaped by social evolution, for the real origins of the state
in both its structural and its psychological aspects.   As
a necessary corollary, the state is looked upon as having
evolved as a social institution, becoming gradually, if
imperfectly, adapted to the needs of a developing society.

[4] Cf. Cole, op. cit.; also Laski, *Studies in the Problem of Sovereignty.*
[5] Cf. Bentley, *The Process of Government;* Ratzenhofer,
Wesen und Zweck der Politik; Small, *General Sociology.*
[6] Cf. Cole, op. cit.; Carpenter, *Guild Socialism.*
[7] Cf. Ward, *Dynamic Sociology;* Hobhouse, *Social Evolution
and Political Theory;* Giddings, *The Responsible State.*

This has led to an altered conception of the relations of society, state and government. The so-called "social hypothesis" has now won well-nigh universal triumph.[8] Society appears as the general matrix out of which the state evolves as a specialized organ or agency, while the government is viewed in its relation to the state as the delegated agent of the state, which acts for the principal. Much of the newer theory contends that a considerable number of the concrete functions of government will be carried on outside the pale and oversight of the state and under the supervision of various specialized communities and functional associations, of which the neighborhood group and the trade-union are the most frequently emphasized.[9]

As to the form of government best adapted to a society, the principle of relativity prevails; that is to say, there is no absolutely "best" government. The desirable type of government is that which is best suited to the needs of the existing society at a particular time. Unusual circumstances, especially such crises as wars, will entail changes in governmental pressure and machinery which, in spite of no change in the legal classification, really constitute a fundamental, if temporary, alteration of the form of government. In other words, social conditions not only determine the normal and prevailing type of government, but also bring about what are at times revolutionary changes to meet the stress of extraordinary conditions

---

[8] Even Ford admits this, though he will have nothing to do with the sociological analysis which brought this hypothesis into being; cf. his *The Natural History of the State,* pp. 146–9.

[9] Cf. the works of Cole, Laski, MacIver, Follett as cited; also Geddes and Branford, *The Coming Polity.*

or occurrences.[10]   Though there is now a general agreement that democracy is best adapted to the needs of present-day society, it is no revered shibboleth, but is regarded as probably the least defective of the available forms of political control.

Democracy, however, is held to mean something far more than the granting of universal suffrage ; it implies a type of society, a form of state and a particular mechanism of government.   Its vindication as a final development in political machinery is by no means assured.   Its success depends upon the existence of certain essential conditions, physical and cultural, in the society where it is introduced.   In fact, some critical writers of by no means reactionary tendencies would question the major premise of the fundamental equality of man which underlies the dogmas and practices of democracy, and suggest that democracy is bound to disappear as a hopeless and discredited political experiment unless some more effective means is devised for insuring a greater degree of capable leadership than has thus far been discovered.[11] The machinery of political control is now looked upon as an organic whole and not as a series of contending departments or divisions arrayed against one another in a formidable system of checks and balances.   Montesquieu's venerable theory has given way under doctrinal criticism and practical experiment until it has come to be looked up-

[10] Cf. Giddings, *The Responsible State;* also his "Pluralistic Behavior," in *American Journal of Sociology,* Vol. XXV, pp. 385–404, 539–61.
[11] Cf. Faguet, *The Cult of Incompetence;* McDougall, *Is America Safe for Democracy?*

on as an historical inaccuracy, and an anachronistic administrative monstrosity.[12]

The sovereignty of the state is in no sense a sanctified metaphysical power; it is simply social pressure exerted through particular channels in support of existing political institutions and delegated agents of authority, and is based far more upon custom and tradition than upon reasoned analysis and conscious approval. Its alleged qualities of originality, universality, absoluteness and lack of finite limitations have long since been dissolved under criticism, and now even its quality of unity is challenged.[13] Still others doubt its essential reality, and claim that nothing more than political authority, limited sharply by the interdependence of modern national states, can be postulated or established. They would further doubt, indeed, whether any determinate political superior can be identified in the mazes and fluctuations of social pressure. In short, the whole problem of sovereignty is one for broad sociological and psychological analysis and not for microscopic examination by lawyers.

With respect to liberty, while political scientists may still admit that, for purposes of preliminary definition, liberty may be regarded as secured, defined and limited by law, yet they believe that social forces, expressing group approval or disapproval, are much more vital than formal legal enactments. In other words, custom, education and class interests and ambitions have far more influence upon

[12] Cf. Goodnow, *Politics and Administration;* Powell, *"The Separation of Powers," Political Science Quarterly,* Vols. XXVII–XXVIII; Ford, *Rise and Growth of American Politics.*
[13] Cf. the works of Laski, Duguit, and Cole as cited.

the chief phases of human conduct than the formal commands or prohibitions of the state. Probably less than a tenth of the inhibitions in the daily conduct of the individual, which constitute the real limitations upon personal liberty, are the product of the law. But beyond all this is the significant fact, so ably emphasized by Roscoe Pound, that all vital law is a product of society, created by social interests and generally obeyed only when supported by public opinion. Similarly, individual rights have come to be investigated from the social angle. No such thing as the abstract isolated individual is known to social science. Nor are individual rights metaphysical entities. They are but concrete lines and types of sanctioned action essential to the orderly and efficient functioning of the social organism as a whole; and as such they are originated, determined, defined and limited by social interests and necessity. The rights of man are in no sense primordial abstractions to which society has to adjust itself and for the protection of which the state was specifically created.[14]

With respect to the problem of state activity, the conception of the state as a collective policeman, which characterized the legalistic political theory, has been completely overthrown. The majority of writers now hold that social interest is the only limitation which can be placed upon state activity and the only criterion by which it can be adequately guided. Constructive social legislation, directed by the principles of social science, however much delegated to functional groups in administra-

[14] Cf. Pound, *The Spirit of the Common Law; Interpretations of Legal History;* and numerous articles; also Giddings, *The Responsible State;* Hobhouse, *The Elements of Social Justice.*

tion, is looked upon as only the consciously collective mode of furthering social progress.[15] Some more advanced writers would limit the powers of the state to control over the consumers' interests in society, but even in this field they would assign powers to the state which would have made Bentham, Cobden or Austin gasp with astonishment.

The old view of the national state as the final stage of political evolution has largely disappeared. The size of the state appears to be a function of social evolution, so that the national state is but an important stage in the evolution of political aggregates which in due time will be replaced by leagues and federations of states, and ultimately, perhaps, by a world-state. Already the vital interdependence of states is recognized, and the extensive limitations upon the alleged absolute sovereignty of the national state are frankly acknowledged.[16]

Even more significant than the above has been the tendency on the part of recent writers on politics to deal more thoroughly and extensively with extra-legal aspects of political problems. The significance of public opinion has come to be more fully recognized and more profoundly analyzed. It is seen to be no metaphysical and transcendental super-individual entity, but rather that general organization and expression of the psychic force of the community which is given content and direction by custom, tradition, conventional education and other non-intellectual factors, or is deliberately shaped by the con-

[15] Cf. Goodnow, *Social Reform and the Constitution;* Freund, *Standards of American Legislation;* Brown, *The Underlying Principles of Modern Legislation;* also the works of such sociologists as Ward, Hobhouse, Stein, Small, and Schäffle.

[16] Cf. Novicow, *Les luttes entre sociétés humaines;* De Greef,

scious and artful propaganda of the "vested interests."
Yet, whatever its defects, it is the most powerful force
which supports and directs public authority; hence the
importance of improving public opinion and making its
content and operation progressively more the product of
the true intellectual aristocracy rather than of the archaic
and irrational force of custom or the sinister and selfish
manipulation of ascendant classes.[17]

Political parties are no longer looked upon as merely
extra-legal entities not contemplated by the constitution,
or unselfish philanthropic organizations devoted to advancing the interests of the country as a whole, but as
organizations centering about a set of distinct interests for
which they desire to obtain public recognition, aid and protection. These "interest-groups" may be specific and
highly articulate, as in the case of well-known labor or
agrarian parties; or they may be general and inclusive, as
in the Conservative and Liberal party alignment in Great
Britain. Even in the United States, where the major
parties have long since ceased to have any *rationale* except an organized effort to exploit the public and bear no
real outward relation to the vital issues of the day, the
dominant interests are able to find effective, if indirect and
surreptitious, modes of utilizing the party machinery for
the advancement of their special aims and interests.[18]

La structure générale des sociétés; also the writings of Hob-
house, Vaccaro, Hobson, Giddings, and others.
   [17] Cf. Lippmann, *Public Opinion;* Cooley, *Social Organization;*
Ross, *Social Control;* Wallas, *Human Nature in Politics;* Tarde,
Les transformations du pouvoir; Lowell, *Public Opinion and
Popular Government;* and *Public Opinion in War and Peace.*
   [18] Cf. Michels, *Political Parties;* Bentley, *The Process of
Government;* Brooks, *Corruption in American Politics and Life;*
Schlesinger, *New Viewpoints in American History,* Chap. XII.

Particularly important in this field of the analysis of extra-legal phases of politics is the growing attention given to the vital sources and organs of social control and social self-control. This tendency was noted above in the brief reference to the modern notions of the origins of the state and the nature of sovereignty. It has been cheerfully conceded by all progressive political scientists that the whole problem of political obedience and of the social forms or institutions which are created to give specific character to individual subordination and group discipline, is one which must be handed over to the sociologists and the psychologists, individual and social, for analysis and solution.[19]

Finally, the approach to the history of political theory has been modified by the sociological orientation. It is held that no analysis of the political theory of an individual or a particular school, however refined and voluminous, can in any way be regarded as adequate unless it gives a comprehensive picture of the social and economic environment which is reflected in the body of doctrine. In other words, the social determination of political theory, as well as of political institutions, has been accepted.[20] In fact, the more progressive students of politics complain when even formal analytical treatments of public law are based solely upon an analysis of written

[19] Cf. Wallas, op. cit.; Trotter, *Instincts of the Herd in Peace and War;* Sumner, *Folkways.*

[20] Cf. Giddings, "Concepts and Methods of Sociology," in *American Journal of Sociology,* Vol. X, pp. 166 ff., and his "A Theory of Social Causation," in *Publications of the American Economic Association,* third series, Vol. V, No. 2, pp. 139–74, esp. pp. 172-74; also Laski, "The Literature of Politics," in *The New Republic,* Nov. 17, 1917.

constitutions, legal documents and judicial decisions, and
do not subject to scrutiny the actual operation of the
political system and the basic social and economic forces
which are brought to a focus in the political struggles
and transformations.[21]

This brief and incomplete review of the changed orientation in political science will to some extent, at least, indicate the influence of the sociological point of view in
this field.   As Small has well said: [22]

> The only possible vindication for an intellectual movement
> is that people after a while find themselves thinking its
> way.   It is as evident that all thinking about social rela-
> tions is setting irresistibly towards sociological channels, as
> that all our thinking is affected by Darwin.   The solemn
> men who return from reading the signs of the times with
> reports that there is nothing in sociology, deserve a stanza
> in the old song of Noah's neighbors: They knew it wasn't
> going to be much of a shower.

Of course, no one would be foolish enough to contend that this broader approach to political problems is
ultra-modern or that it is the unique contribution of sociology.   Almost from the beginning of politics there have
been writers who have stressed the social, economic and
psychological background of political phenomena.[23]   Aristotle's analysis of the psychological and economic factors
in political institutions; Machiavelli's psychological study

[21] Cf. Beard, article in *Political Science Quarterly*, Vol. XXV,
p. 534.
[22] *American Journal of Sociology*, Vol. XV, pp. 14–15.
[23] These facts are assembled in Dunning's *History of Political
Theories*, and Merriam's *History of American Political Theories*.
Cf. also the stimulating review in Beard's *The Economic Basis
of Politics*.

of leadership; Bodin's crude attempt to work out the physical and psychic foundations of politics; Althusius' emphasis on the group as the basis of social and political life; Harrington's views on the importance of property and mental capacity in political activity and policies; Montesquieu's notion of political relativity, founded upon a sociological view of the factors creating and shaping the state; Ferguson's anticipation of Gumplowicz in tracing the historical origins of the state; the economic interpretation of politics brought forward by the Ricardian Socialists; Hamilton's contention that the raw material of politics was to be sought in the facts of human nature and not in "musty parchments"; the keen analysis of the part played by property in determining political alignments, contained in the writings of Adams, Madison, Webster and Calhoun; and the contention of Calhoun that representative government should be based to a considerable extent upon the recognition of these economic interest-groups—these are but some of the more conspicuous earlier examples of a fundamentally sociological approach to the study and analysis of political phenomena.

For a half-century, however, this tendency was retarded by the influence of the lawyers upon political theory and practice. So far did this go that we find so eminent a political scientist as John W. Burgess declaring:[24] "I do not hesitate to call the governmental system of the United States the aristocracy of the robe, and I do not hesitate to pronounce this the truest aristocracy for the purposes of government which the world has yet produced." Even formal political science was for the

[24] Political Science, Vol. II, p. 365. (Cited by Merriam in his *American Political Ideas,* p. 155.) Cf. Brooks, op. cit.

most part dominated by the abstract legalistic methods and concepts of the Austinian analytical jurisprudence and the German *Staatsrechtslehre*. Perhaps that which is most to the credit of this school is the cheerful frankness with which its members have admitted that their doctrines have nothing in common with those of the sociological school. The writer does not in any way mean to imply that the sociological postulates cannot be harmonized with the viewpoint of the student of jurisprudence; it is not a matter of sociology versus law, but of sociology versus the type of law represented by the political doctrines of the metaphysical jurists or of the Supreme Court of the United States as in the case of *Lochner v. New York* or of the *Hitchman Coal and Coke Company v. Mitchell*. Indeed, some of the most significant and helpful impulses to the sociological orientation have come from such lawyers as Gierke, Maitland, Duguit, Pound, Freund, and Goodnow, and from judges such as Harlan, Holmes, Brandeis, Hand, G. W. Anderson, Cardoza, and others.

What sociology has done for political science is not to originate the synthetic approach to politics, but rather to put the lawyers of the metaphysical and "mechanical" schools to rout and to restore the viewpoint of Ferguson, Hall, Madison and Calhoun. Indeed, it has done more than to restore this general view-point; it has strengthened and modernized it through an infusion of Darwinian biology and dynamic psychology. It would be futile to discuss the problem of whether this change has been due to sociological influences alone or to that general alteration of method and attitude that has accompanied the gradual development of sociology. Be that as it may, one cannot well escape from the conviction that it has been a product of the triumph of the "sociological movement," for there was certainly nothing in Austin which would lead directly to Pound and little in Laband or Jellinek which would bring forth the doctrines of Wallas, Ratzenhofer, Bentley, Laski, Duguit, Krabbe or Beard.

We may now turn to an analysis of the nature of sociology and its relation to political science, and then to a brief survey of the major contributions of sociological writers to various problems of political science.

CHAPTER II

1. *Nature of Sociology*

Of all the problems connected with the contributions of sociology to political theory, none is more important, complicated, or controverted than the question of the nature and scope of sociology and its relation to political science.

As a definition of sociology, that of Giddings is probably unexcelled for brevity and clarity: [1]

Sociology is an attempt to account for the origin, growth, structure, and activities of society by the operation of physical, vital, and psychical causes, working together in a process of evolution.

Small's definition may be offered as a clear statement of the group orientation of sociological analysis: [2]

The sociological technique is that variant among the social science techniques which proceeds from the perception that, after allowing for their purely physical relations, all human phenomena are functions not only of persons, but of persons whose personality on the one hand expresses itself in part

[1] *Principles of Sociology,* p. 8. Cf. also Ellwood, *Sociology in its Psychological Aspects,* pp. 8, 15.
[2] Article on "Sociology," in *Encyclopedia Americana.*

through the formation of groups, and on the other hand is in part produced through the influence of groups. In brief, sociology is that technique which approaches knowledge of human experience as a whole through investigation of group-aspects of the phenomena.

Employing as its basic equipment the accepted results of the organic, physical and psychological sciences, sociology attempts to analyze the social process as a whole and aims at the attainment of a thorough and accurate knowledge of the process of association in its most general and fundamental aspects. It maintains as its most vital thesis that this generalized knowledge of the social process furnishes the indispensable basis and the common point of orientation of the special social sciences.[3]

To this extent all sociologists of any prominence are agreed. The main point of disagreement, in theory, at least, is in regard to the method by which this generalized knowledge of the social process is to be obtained. Those who hold with Giddings that sociology is the elemental social science, contend that it reaches its desired goal by analyzing and coordinating the laws and processes of the physical, vital and psychological sciences and by applying these results through an investigation of society as a unified whole. It deals with the origin, classification and analysis of the stimuli and responses in society in their totality and with the investigation of the varieties of social activity and organization which grow out of them. The differentiation, further analysis and final application and testing of these generalizations are the prerogative and the function of the special social sciences, which may

[3] Cf. Giddings, op. cit., Chap. II; also Small, *The Meaning of Social Science*, passim.

well be as important and complicated as sociology, but which must use the latter as a common starting-point.[4]

On the other hand, those who support the views of Small and the majority of German sociologists, maintain that sociology can arrive at an accurate conception of the associative process as a whole only by organizing and co-ordinating the accepted results of the special social sciences.[5] It is obvious, however, that both of these contentions and methods are valid and indispensable, and are mutually supplementary. Indeed, it is probable that neither group of theorists would deny the value of the opinions of the other, but rather disagree as to the amount of emphasis which should be attached to the one or the other of the methods of approach to the sociological analysis of the social process.[6]

2. *Relation of Sociology to the Special Social Sciences*

The question of the relation of sociology to the special social sciences, which embrace political science, economics, history, jurisprudence, ethics, and social psychology, has furnished the basis of some of the warmest debates to which the recent development of sociology has given rise, and is not yet settled in a conclusive manner.

It was inevitable that this problem should involve heated discussions and numerous clashes, since it was at this point that the "pretensions" of sociology came into the most direct conflict with those of the older and better es-

[4] Cf. Giddings, op. cit., pp. 31, 33; also his *Descriptive and Historical Sociology*, pp. 3–9, 124–8, 135–6, 176–85, 331–4.

[5] Cf. Small, op. cit.; also his article in *American Journal of Sociology*, Vol. II, pp. 288 ff.; and his *General Sociology*, pp. 26–27 et passim.

[6] Cf. Ellwood, op. cit., pp. 29–32.

tablished special social sciences. The controversy was further complicated by the fact that, not only were the representatives of sociology and the special social sciences at variance over the boundary between their respective disciplines, but there failed to be any general agreement among the sociologists themselves in regard to the nature and scope of their subject.[7]

The tension created by the disagreement was doubtless intensified by the fact that Auguste Comte, the founder of formal sociology, contended that the special social sciences had no valid claim to a separate existence, and proposed to absorb them all in a unitary science of social phenomena.[8] It is not surprising, therefore, that the representatives of the special social sciences have viewed with alarm and repugnance the rise of this "interloper," which not only dared to question their traditional supremacy, but even presumed to deny their right to existence.

Out of the controversies of the last three quarters of a century, however, and along with the further development of sociology and a modification of its claims, there has come about a better understanding between sociologists and special social scientists, until at present there is little friction between the more enlightened representatives of each.[9] On the one hand, there is a recognition of the

[7] Cf. Giddings' view of the opinions of Small in his *Principles of Sociology,* p. 12, note; and Small's retort, *American Journal of Sociology,* Vol. II, pp. 288 ff.

[8] Cf. Martineau, *The Positive Philosophy of Comte,* Vol. I, pp. 140-1, 218, 258; Vol. II, pp. 210-22; Vol. III, pp. 383-5; also Giddings, op. cit., p. 28.

[9] There has been an occasional recrudescence of the virulence of the past, the most conspicuous examples of which are to be found in the articles of H. J. Ford in the *American Journal of Sociology,* Vol. XV, pp. 96 ff., 244 ff.

fact that their respective fields cannot be parcelled out with delicate precision until both sociology and the special social sciences have carried their researches much further; and, on the other hand, there has been a growth of the laudable tendency to recognize that cooperation is much more likely than controversy to be of productive advantage to both parties.[10]

Attention may now be directed to a survey of the main conceptions of the relation of sociology to the special social sciences which have been held by sociologists and the academic world.

The Comtian conception has already been described. At present it has few if any adherents except among the dwindling group of Comte's followers. Certainly no reputable sociologist of today would give his assent to any such solution of the problem. Equally without support

[10] The general spirit of cooperation, conscious or unconscious, on the part of the special social scientists is to be seen in the work of economists such as Ely, Clark, Commons, Patten, Fetter, Hobson, Gide, Schmoller, and Loria; of political scientists such as Goodnow, Beard, Bentley, Merriam, Bryce, and Faguet; of jurists such as Holmes, Pound, and Gierke; of historians such as Green, Rambaud, McMaster, Lamprecht, Vinogradoff, Maitland, Robinson, Turner, Shotwell, Slater, Marvin, Seignobos, and the economic historians; of students of ethics such as Dewey and Stephens; and of social psychologists such as Baldwin, McDougall, Wallas, Le Bon, Wundt, and Sighele. Examples of the reciprocal activity of sociologists in contributing to the special social sciences may be discerned in the encyclopedic interests of Comte and Spencer; in the contributions of Giddings to economics and political science; of Sumner, Tarde, Simmel, Hobhouse, Durkheim, and Kovalevsky to anthropology; of Tarde to jurisprudence and criminology; of Hobhouse and Hayes to ethics; of Novicow, De Greef, Ross, Gumplowicz, Ratzenhofer, Small and the social economists to political science; of Ellwood, Ross, Cooley, Tarde, and Durkheim to social psychology.

among reputable sociologists is the popular conception that has gained vogue on account of a doubtful library classification which represents sociology as the body or *corpus* of the social sciences, thus making the terms sociology and social science synonymous.[11] Another erroneous popular conception of sociology is that which regards it as the science of social evils or social pathology.

Turning now to the more generally accepted views of the relation of sociology to the special social sciences, the proposition that sociology is a philosophical synthesis of the special social sciences, which attempts to organize their results into a "coherent social philosophy," has the sanction of a large number of the most eminent sociologists. This was essentially the view of Herbert Spencer,[12] and it has, with due allowance for individual variations in definition, received the assent of Schäffle,[13] Stein,[14] Barth,[15] Tönnies,[16] and Ratzenhofer [17] in Germany; of Tarde [18] and Worms [19] in France; of the Belgian, De

[11] Durkheim's use of a scheme closely allied to this conception in arranging the material in *L'année sociologique* is adopted primarily as a matter of convenience, although he is more inclined to favor this conception than any other sociologist; cf. *Sociological Papers*, 1904, pp. 197–200, 258–80.

[12] *Principles of Sociology*, Vol. I, pp. 424–32.

[13] *Bau und Leben des sozialen Körpers*, Vol. I, p. 1.

[14] *Die soziale Frage im Lichte der Philosophie*, 3 u. 4 Auflage, 1923, pp. 1–47; *Einführung in die Soziologie*, pp. 11–18; and *Sociological Papers*, 1904, pp. 245–47.

[15] *Die Philosophie der Geschichte als Soziologie*, pp. 10–12; *Sociological Papers*, 1904, pp. 217–18.

[16] *Sociological Papers*, 1904, pp. 250–51.

[17] *Die soziologische Erkenntniss*, p. 6; *Soziologie*, pp. 2–3.

[18] *La revue internationale de sociologie*, Vol. XII, pp. 84–7.

[19] *Sociological Papers*, 1904, p. 254; *Philosophie des sciences sociales*, Vol. I, pp. 208–11.

Greef;[20] of the Russians, Novicow[21] and Roberty;[22] of the Italian, Cosentini;[23] and of Small in America, who has been the most ardent and effective exponent of this position.[24]

Another conception, which finds extensive support among sociologists, is that sociology is not the philosophical synthesis of the special social sciences, but is the fundamental or elemental social science, which is the common basis or starting-point of the special social sciences. It furnishes those fundamental generalizations regarding social phenomena upon which any special social science must found its more intensive investigations, thus bearing much the same relation to social science that arithmetic and algebra bear to mathematics, or that mathematics and physics bear to the engineering sciences. This view of the nature of sociology, which has been the most vigorously defended by Giddings,[25] is supported by Sumner,[26] Ellwood,[27] Ross,[28] Stuckenberg,[29] and Gumplowicz.[30]

Another important group of sociologists emphasize the fact that sociology is primarily a method of approach to

[20] *La structure générale des sociétés,* Vol. I, pp. 7-8.

[21] *Les luttes entre sociétés humaines,* pp. 531, 636.

[22] *La sociologie,* pp. 112–15.

[23] *Sociological Papers,* 1904, pp. 225–6.

[24] *An Introduction to the Study of Society,* pp. 54, 62; *General Sociology,* pp. 26–7; *The Meaning of Social Science.*

[25] *Principles of Sociology,* Chap. II.

[26] *War and Other Essays,* pp. 167–92.

[27] *Sociology in its Psychological Aspects,* pp. 8, 15, 29 f.

[28] *Foundations of Sociology,* pp. 6–7, 27–8.

[29] *Introduction to the Study of Sociology,* pp. 77–83; *Sociology,* Vol. I, pp. 17–21, 41.

[30] *Outlines of Sociology,* p. 90.

the study of social phenomena. Hobhouse states this view very concisely:[31]

Properly considered, General Sociology is neither a separate science complete in itself before specialism begins, nor is it a mere synthesis of the social sciences consisting in a mechanical juxtaposition of their results. It is rather a vitalising principle that runs through all social investigation, nourishing and nourished by it in turn, stimulating inquiry, correlating results, exhibiting the life of the whole in the parts, and returning from the study of the parts to a fuller comprehension of the whole.

This view of the problem has been commended by Durkheim,[32] Hayes,[33] and Simmel,[34] and is given consideration by Small and Thomas in their latest writings.

In addition to these groups of opinions there are certain distinctly individual doctrines, of which perhaps the most conspicuous is that of Ward, who maintains that, while sociology draws its data from the special social sciences, it is not their sum, but, like a chemical compound, is a new product. It is, to adopt Ward's terminology, a "creative synthesis."[35]

Again, the views of the nature and relations of sociology have had somewhat of a distinctly national line of cleavage.[36] In the United States, which has been most productive in the field of sociological theory, so-

[31] *Sociological Review,* 1908, Vol. I, p. 8.
[32] *Sociological Papers,* 1904, pp. 197–200, 258–80. Cf. also Gehlke, *Emile Durkheim's Contributions to Sociology,* Chap. V.
[33] *Introduction to the Study of Sociology,* pp. 4–8.
[34] "The Problem of Sociology" in *Annals of American Academy of Political and Social Science,* Vol. VI, pp. 412–23.
[35] *Pure Sociology,* p. 91; *American Journal of Sociology,* Vol. VII, p. 636.
[36] Cf. Ross, *Foundations of Sociology,* pp. 275–85.

ciology has been mainly regarded as a fundamental social science and has received systematic exposition from
this point of view. In France it has been, in the main,
identified with the theory of the social organism and with
social psychology. In Germany the chief emphasis has
been put upon sociology as a philosophy of history, as
social economics, or as an analysis of group conflict. In
England, again, the sociological movement has been mainly
identified with ethnology and with the development of
eugenics and more general biological theories. Russian
sociologists, reflecting the peasant constitution of Russian society, have emphasized mutual aid and cooperation
as the basic factors in society, and have tended to deal
extensively with schemes of social reconstruction. In
Italy and Spain sociology has been chiefly limited to exposition of existing sociological thought.

Finally, the matter is further complicated by the fact
that many sociologists support more than one solution of
the problem. For example, Small, who is the most prominent American exponent of the view that sociology is
the synthetic philosophy of the special social sciences, is
also one of the leading contributors to the study of sociological method. Hobhouse, Durkheim, Simmel, Barth,
and Ratzenhofer are other examples of writers who hold
more than one view of the nature and relations of sociology. In general, however, the three main conceptions
of sociology which receive the assent of the great majority of sociologists are those which regard sociology as (1)
a philosophical synthesis of the special social sciences, as
(2) the fundamental social science, or lastly as (3) a
broader and sounder method of studying social phenomena. A theory which deviates from all three of these

views must be regarded as an individual opinion rather than as a sanctioned professional judgment.[37]   The most significant aspect common to all of these opinions is that none of them attempts to engulf or eliminate any of the special social sciences, but all agree upon the value of the latter and the necessity for their vigorous independent existence.

3. *Relation of Sociology to Political Science*

Whatever may be the differences of opinion in regard to the abstract question of the relation of sociology to the special social sciences, there seems to be a general agreement among sociologists as to the specific relation of sociology to political science with respect to the approach to the study of political phenomena.

Sociology is primarily concerned with the evolution of the political community, which political science assumes to be existent, and with the development and functioning of all the organs of social control, of which the state is only the most prominent among many.   It is also immediately interested in the modifications effected by the organs of social control, among them the state, in the structure of society.   Political science, assuming the existence of the state, concentrates its attention upon an analysis of the state and the mechanism of government, and is only indirectly concerned with the broader problems of social origins, structure, and functioning, or with the reaction of

[37] For important presentations of the argument that these different views are supplementary rather than in vital conflict, cf. Ellwood, op. cit., pp. 29-64; also Vincent, in *American Journal of Sociology*, Vol. X, p. 158.

the state upon society. Sociology must derive from political science its knowledge of the details of political
organization and activities, while political science can
avoid becoming metaphysical only by accepting as its pro-
legomena the sociological generalizations with respect to
the underlying foundations of law and political institutions.[38] Giddings thus emphasizes this important but generally disregarded truth: [39]

To teach the theory of the state to men who have not
learned the first principles of sociology, is like teaching
astronomy or thermodynamics to men who have not learned
the Newtonian laws of motion.

Commons holds that: [40]

Society precedes the state just as it precedes the family,
the church, the corporation, the political party. It unites
all of these as a tree unites its branches.

The state is the coercive institution of society. It is not

[38] Cf. Giddings, *Principles of Sociology*, p. 37; also *Political
Science Quarterly*, Vol. XXIV, pp. 571-72.

[39] *Principles of Sociology*, pp. 33, 37. Cf. also Small, *General
Sociology*, pp. 226 ff.; and Hobhouse, *Sociological Review*, Vol.
I, pp. 4-9.—This is also the view of the more enlightened and
advanced political scientists. Cf. Willoughby, *The Nature of the
State*, pp. 1-7; Dunning, *A History of Political Theories, Ancient
and Medieval*, Introduction, pp. xvii-xxii; Bryce, *Sociological
Papers*, 1904, pp. xii-xviii, 223-4; Merriam, *History of American
Political Theories*, pp. 329-32; and *American Political Ideas,
1865-1917*, pp. 405 ff.—The most conspicuous examples of the
survival of the pre-sociological views of a century ago are to
be found in the articles of H. J. Ford, *American Journal of
Sociology*, Vol. XV, pp. 96 ff.; 244 ff.; in his *Natural History of
the State*, esp. pp. 146-9; also in the article of H. G. Wells,
"The So-called Science of Sociology," in *Sociological Papers*,
1906, pp. 357-69.

[40] *American Journal of Sociology*, Vol. V, pp. 3, 359.

an ideal entity, superimposed on society, but is an accumulated series of compromises between social classes, each seeking to secure for itself control over the coercive elements which exist implicitly in society with the institution of private property.

Ellwood thus expresses this dependence of political science upon sociology: [41]

The phenomena of governmental authority and control, and of political organization, however important they may be, are comparatively late developments in social evolution. Therefore, before authority and control as manifested in the state can be understood, social organization and the nature of society in general must be understood. Political science must depend, therefore, for its knowledge of the origins of authority and subordination, of social control, and of the springs of political organization, upon the general science which deals with the whole theory of society, that is, sociology.

[41] *Sociology in its Psychological Aspects,* pp. 36-7.

CHAPTER III

1. *Inadequate Characterizations of the Sociological Conception of the State*

At the outset it seems necessary to clear away certain conceptions of the sociological methods of approach to political problems which, whatever their accuracy as regards earlier stages in the development of sociology, are quite misleading as descriptive of the present status of sociological investigation. In his excellent and comprehensive *Introduction to Political Science,* J. W. Garner says of the sociological approach to politics: [1]

The so-called sociological method considers the state primarily as a social organism, whose component parts are individuals, and seeks to deduce its qualities and attributes from the qualities and attributes of the men composing it. It seeks to interpret the life of the state by applying to it the theory of evolution in the same way that the growth of the individual is explained by evolution.

This is an excellent statement of the attitude of the so-called organismic or biological school of sociologists, whose contributions to political science have been admirably

[1] Op. cit., pp. 23–4.

summarized by F. W. Coker;[2] but the organismic school is now held to represent one of the least important and certainly the most archaic of the types of sociological doctrine. Even those writers who approach sociological questions from the biological viewpoint have ceased almost entirely to employ the partially misleading and essentially sterile terminology of the biological analogy.[3]

In a brilliant and suggestive article on "Political Science in the Crucible," Charles A. Beard, after correctly calling attention to the fact that "political science in this country has always been under bondage to the lawyers," also complains that sociology has done little to commute or alleviate this fatal servitude and holds that it has merely "wandered around in the dim vastness of classified emotions, touching neither the substantial borders of the state, on the one hand, nor the equally tangible structures of commerce or industry, on the other."[4] This characterization might well apply to the Kidd-Sutherland stage and type of sociological theory, or to the first works of some later sociologists, but it is a most incomplete description of the totality of sociological achievements in this field. The fact is, indeed, that the classified emotions have not attracted much specific attention from the sociologists. The remainder of this work will serve to show that Beard's somewhat typical view of sociology is rather over-gloomy, and that many, if not most, of the works which he and his fellow liberals in political science hail

[2] *Organismic Theories of the State,* pp. 115–90. Cf. also Towne, *Die Auffassung der Gesellschaft als Organismus.*
[3] E. g., Ammon, Schallmayer, Vacher de Lapouge, Carr-Saunders, Holmes, Conklin, Pearson, Hankins, Tenney, and Keller.
[4] *The New Republic,* Nov. 7, 1917.

as harbingers of the new era in political theory—such
books as Bentley's *Process of Government,* Michels'
Political Parties, Oppenheimer's *The State,* Wallas' *Human
Nature in Politics, The Great Society,* and *Our Social
Heritage,* and Lippmann's *Preface to Politics*—are either
avowed sociological products or are alone made possible
by the acceptance of the sociological concepts and methods
of the last quarter of a century.

2. *The State and the Social Organism*

Probably the first definite group of sociologists to formulate specific theories of the state were those who made
wide use of the biological or organic analogy.   The great
differences in the political environments in which they
formulated their views led, however, to a considerable
divergence in opinion as to the real nature and function
of the state.   Lilienfeld,[5] Schäffle,[6] and Worms,[7] looked
upon the state as the brain or the controlling and directing apparatus of the social organism, with no limitations
upon its powers except the function of forwarding the
welfare of the society.   The more highly developed the
society or the state, the greater the amount of state activity which might be expected and which would be legitimate and beneficial.   Fouillée,[8] while introducing psychological considerations and denying a perfect analogy between the state and the brain of the social organism, stood

[5] *Gedanken über die Socialwissenschaft der Zukunft,* esp. Vol.
I, pp. 81–92, 116–9, 186–8.
[6] *Bau und Leben des socialen Körpers,* Vol. I, pp. 170–5; Vol.
II, pp. 427–591.
[7] *Organisme et société,* pp. 37 ff.
[8] *La science sociale contemporaine,* Bks. III–V.

with Lilienfeld, Schäffle, and Worms in magnifying the
importance of the state as the directive organ of society;
in fact, he practically identified the state with the social
organism.   Spencer [9] believed the state to be analogous to
the brain in the individual organism, but he deduced from
this premise a quite different conclusion as regards the
functions and dignity of the state.   Its controlling and
directing activity was to be limited to that "negative regulation" which would insure to each individual the direct results of his own nature and conduct—in other
words, to defense against foreign enemies and to protection from robbery and exploitation by fellow-citizens.
Finally, in the works of Novicow [10] one finds the most extreme individualistic position held by the biological school.
He contends that the state is in no sense the brain of the
social organism, but that this position in society is to
be assigned to the intellectual aristocracy.   If anything,
he is more severe than Spencer in his limitations upon
legitimate state activity.

3. *The State and the Psychic Personality of the Group*

A position intermediate between the biological and the
psychological theories of the state is held by Gierke and
Maitland, whose point of view is shared by such writers
as Figgis, Laski and Duguit.   The founder of this position was the German jurist, Johannes Althusius, who began to write at the close of the sixteenth century.   His

[9] *Principles of Sociology*, Vol. I, Pt. II; *Man versus the
State*, pp. 401–11. *Principles of Ethics*, Pt. IV.
[10] *Les luttes entre sociétés humaines*, pp. 335, 355, 494, 604;
Conscience et volonté sociales, pp. 23, 237–8.

theory of the state as a hierarchy of constituent groups
was broadened out by his modern interpreter, Otto Gierke,
in his *Genossenschaftslehre,* which was sponsored and
clarified by the eminent English historian and jurist, F.
W. Maitland. Briefly, the doctrine is that the state is
not a collection of individuals but an aggregation of groups.
These groups, in turn, are not merely a plural number of
individuals, but an organization of individuals designed
to achieve a definite purpose. As purposive groups they
are psychic organisms, possessing not a fictitious but a
real psychic personality. The state exists as the general
political organization of society for the purpose of adjusting the relation of these groups to one another and
of each and all of them to the state. The exponents of
this doctrine of the reality and significance of the group
range in their interpretation of the place and significance
of the state all the way from the position of such writers
as Ernest Barker, who support an Aristotelian-Hegelian
adulation of the state, to the extreme pluralists and the
Syndicalists, who would eliminate the state altogether.[11]

4. *The State as the Supreme Human Association*

Representatives of the characteristic theories of the
state may be discovered among later systematic sociolo-

[11] Cf. Althusius, *Politica methodice digesta;* Gierke, *Das Genossenschaftsrecht* and *Die Genossenschaftstheorie;* Maitland,
Introduction to Gierke's *Political Theories of the Middle Age;*
also *Collected Papers,* Vol. III, pp. 210 ff.; Figgis, *Churches in
the Modern State;* Laski, *Studies in the Problem of Sovereignty;*
Duguit, *Law in the Modern State.*—On the Syndicalist theory of
the state, cf. Mott, "The Political Theory of Syndicalism," in
Political Science Quarterly, Vol. XXXVII, pp. 25-40.

gists. First in order may be put those who, like Ward, Giddings and Hobhouse, are advocates of a view which furnishes a justification for extensive state activity. Probably the most extreme member of this group is Ward, whose famous conception of the state follows: [12]

We thus see that the state, though genetic in its origin, is telic in its method; that it has but one purpose, function, or mission, that of securing the welfare of society; that its mode of operation is that of preventing the anti-social action of individuals; that in doing this it increases the freedom of human action so long as it is not anti-social; that the state is therefore essentially moral or ethical; that its own acts must necessarily be ethical; that being a natural product it must in a large sense be representative; that in point of fact it is always as good as society will permit it to be; that while thus far in the history of society the state has rarely performed acts that tend to advance mankind, it has always been the condition to all achievement, making possible all the social, industrial, artistic, literary, and scientific activities that go on within the state and under its protection. There is no other human institution with which the state can be compared, and yet, in view of all this, it is the most important of all human institutions.

Giddings is scarcely as dithyrambic as Ward; in what is perhaps his best definition he says that: [13]

The chief purposive organization of civil society is the state, through which the social mind dominates the integral community, prescribes forms and obligations to all minor purposive associations, and shapes the social composition. Coordinating all activities and relations, the state maintains

[12] *Pure Sociology,* p. 555.
[13] *Descriptive and Historical Sociology,* p. 509; also *The Responsible State,* Chaps. II–IV.

conditions under which all its subjects may live, as Aristotle
said, "a perfect and self-sufficing life."

While Hobhouse is a vigorous advocate of state activity for social reform, and was the chief sociological
writer in the English Liberal Party before the World
War, he is careful to point out that he in no way accepts
the metaphysical theory of the state, with its claim of
mystic and absolute attributes for the state. In a characteristic passage he contends that:[14]

The state is an association of human beings—with the
exception of the great world churches, the greatest of all
associations. It has no mystic sanctity or authority rendering it superior to morality or emancipating it from the law
by which transgression brings its own retribution in the
lowering of character. It is an association which has its
own special constitution and circumstances, and in the concrete its duties and rights, like the duties and rights of every
other association and every individual, must be judged in
relation to this constitution and to these circumstances.

5. *The State and the Social Process*

One of the most satisfactory views of the nature of
the state held by sociologists is that which has been set
forth most in detail by Ratzenhofer and Small. It
throws more light on the real nature of the social process
which goes on within the state than most other types of
analysis. It is not unrelated to the views of Gierke and
Maitland. Society is viewed as a complex of conflicting

[14] *Democracy and Reaction*, p. 207. Cf. also his *Metaphysical
Theory of the State*. With this group might also be included
Stein; cf. his *Einführung in die Soziologie*, pp. 320 ff.

interest-groups. The function of the state is to impose
the necessary limitations upon this conflict, so that it will
result in social justice and progress rather than in exploitation and anarchy. The conflict of interest-groups
is the vital and dynamic factor in the social process; the
state is merely the essential regulator of these struggles
and adjustments. The following brief citation from
Small's adaptation of Ratzenhofer's doctrines will clearly
indicate their point of view: [15]

The modern State is both a political organization and an
economic system, but it is much more. The State is a
microcosm of the whole human process. . . . The State is
not a rigid entity but a process—"a becoming"—which
changes with the variation of interests of the component
individuals and groups. . . . The various institutions, political, ecclesiastical, professional, industrial, etc., including
the government, are devices, means, gradually brought into
existence to serve interests that develop within the State.
. . . The constant and fundamental rôle of the State is to
bring to bear upon the individuals composing it a certain
power of constraint to secure from them, in all their struggles with each other, the observance of minimum established
limits of struggle. . . . Civic society organized as the State
is composed of individual and group factors, each of which
has in itself certain elements of political independence.
That is, each has interests seemingly distinct from the interests of the others. Each has some degree of impulse to
assert these interests in spite of the others. Thus the State
is a union of disunions, a conciliation of conflicts, a harmony of discords. The State is an arrangement of combinations by which mutually repellant forces are brought

[15] Small, *General Sociology*, pp. 226, 228, 233, 242, 252-53,
332.—For an elaboration of this doctrine and its application to
an analysis of the American government, cf. Bentley, *The Process of Government.*

into some measure of concurrent action. . . . We thus make out the main tendency of civic struggle to be the ultimate harmonization of all interests. This result we call socialization or civilization.

Directly related to the theory of Ratzenhofer and Small with respect to the nature of the state is that of Gumplowicz and Oppenheimer. The latter agree that the state is fundamentally made up of a number of conflicting groups and classes, each with its special interest; but they hold that the state, instead of operating as a conciliating and harmonizing agent, furnishes the authoritative political means of allowing a minority to rule and carry on the economic exploitation of the majority. Gumplowicz phrases this conception as follows: [16]

If nothing but the universal and essential characteristics of every state were incorporated in the definition, an agreement could be easily reached, for there are but two. First, there are certain institutions directed to securing the sovereignty of some over the others; secondly the sovereignty is always exercised by a minority. *A state, therefore, is the organized control of the minority over the majority.* . . . Investigate the cause of any political revolution and the result will prove that social progress is always produced by economic causes. . . . Nature laid the foundations of ethnically composite states in human necessities and sentiments. Human labor being necessary, sympathy with kindred and tribe and deadly hatred of strangers led to foreign wars. So conquest and the satisfaction of needs through the labor of the conquered, essentially the same, though differing in form, is the great theme of human history.

Oppenheimer expresses the same view: [17]

[16] *Outlines of Sociology,* pp. 118, 121, 123.
[17] *The State,* pp. 5, 15.

Every State in history was or is a *State of classes,* a polity of superior and inferior social groups, based upon distinctions either of rank or of property. This phenomenon must, then, be called the "State." . . . What then is the State as a sociological concept? The State, completely in its genesis, essentially and almost completely during the first stages of its existence, is a social institution, forced by a victorious group of men on a defeated group, with the sole purpose of regulating the dominion of the victorious group over the vanquished, and securing itself against revolt from within and attacks from abroad. Teleologically, this dominion had no other purpose than the economic exploitation of the vanquished by the victors.

6. *The State and the Community*

One of the most interesting and significant attempts to describe the nature of the state and to indicate its position in society has been executed by R. M. MacIver. Tönnies, Stein and Baldwin distinguished between genetic and spontaneous social groupings, designated as "communities," and consciously organized or purposive groups, defined as "societies." [18] Giddings has much the same differentiation in mind when he discriminates between component and constituent societies,[19] while Durkheim's distinction between segmentary and functional groups is likewise not unrelated to these notions.[20] MacIver's classification is somewhat more ambitious, and it is of special importance because it furnishes a background, not only for

[18] Tönnies, *Gemeinschaft und Gesellschaft;* Stein, *Die soziale Frage* (French translation, *La question sociale*), pp. 63 ff.; 114–5, 192; Baldwin, *Social and Ethical Interpretations in Mental Development,* p. 503.

[19] *Inductive Sociology,* pp. 182 ff.

[20] *De la division du travail social,* pp. 118–141, 158–217.

the advocates of political pluralism, but also for those who reject extreme pluralistic doctrine and yet admit the importance of groups in modern political and social life and very frankly recognize the necessity of providing for a better method of organizing their relations to each other and to the state than now prevails in most existing societies. He regards society as the most comprehensive and genetic term; it embraces the whole complex of human relationships. The community is the center of spontaneous and voluntary common life; it is the basic, fundamental, positive and creative element in modern civilisation. Associations are purposive organizations designed to achieve some definite aim or end. The state is an association, but it is distinguished from other associations by the scope of its interests and the thoroughness of its organization, as also by its power to use political law and coercive force. While it is primarily regulative, external, negative, and repressive in its operation, it can achieve much in a positive way, provided its relation to communities and other associations is properly recognized and secured in the constitution and legislation. The state should control other associations to the extent of assuring that they serve the interests of the community in the highest possible degree, and at this point its interference should cease. Some associations require a higher degree of state control than now exists, while others need more freedom. The only scientific policy in this respect must be pragmatic and dynamic.[21] On account of the probable significance of this type of analysis in the future of political

[21] MacIver, *Community: a Sociological Study,* esp. Pt. I. See Cole, *Social Theory* for applications.

theory and practice, the essential sections of MacIver's doctrine are here reproduced: [22]

Society, the most general term of all, I intend to use in a universal or generic sense to include every willed relationship of man to man. If, then, we distinguish community, association, and State from society, it must be by delimiting the former as special kinds or aspects of social fact. The essential distinction here involved, one of the utmost importance, is that between community and association.

By a community I mean any area of common life, village, or town, or district, or country, or even wider area. To deserve the name community, the area must be somehow distinguished from further areas, the common life may have some characteristic of its own such that the frontiers of the area have some meaning. All the laws of the cosmos, physical, biological, and psychological, conspire to bring it about that beings who live together shall resemble one another. Wherever men live together they develop in some kind and degree distinctive common characteristics, manners, traditions, modes of speech, and so on. These are the signs and consequences of an effective common life. It will be seen that a community may be part of a wider community, and that all community is a question of degree. For instance, the English residents in a foreign capital often live in an intimate community of their own, as well as in the wider community of the capital. It is a question of the degree and intensity of the common life. The one extreme is the whole world of men, one great but vague and incoherent common life. The other extreme is the small intense community within which the life of an ordinary individual is lived, a tiny nucleus of common life with a sometimes larger, sometimes smaller, and always varying fringe. Yet even the poorest in social relationships is a member in a chain of social contacts which stretches to the world's end.

[22] Ibid., pp. 22–36.

In the infinite series of social relationships which thus arise, we distinguish the nuclei of intenser common life, cities and nations and tribes, and think of them as *par excellence* communities.

An association is an organisation of social beings (or a body of social beings as organised) for the pursuit of some common interest or interests. It is a determinate social unity built upon common purpose. Every end which men seek is more easily attained for all when all whom it concerns unite to seek it, when all cooperate in seeking it. Thus you may have an association corresponding to every possible interest of social beings. Community bubbles into associations permanent and transient, and no student of the actual social life of the present can help being struck by the enormous number of associations of every kind, political, economic, religious, educational, scientific, artistic, literary, recreative, which today more than ever before enrich the communal life.

A community is a focus of social life, the common living of social beings, an association is an organisation of social life, definitely established for the pursuit of one or more common interests. An association is partial, a community is integral. The members of one association may be members of many other and distinct associations. Within a community there may exist not only numerous associations but also antagonistic associations. Men may associate for the least significant or for the most significant of purposes; the association may mean very much or very little to them, it may mean merely the source of a half-yearly dividend, or it may be the guardian of their dearest or highest interests—but community is something wider and freer than even the greatest associations; it is the greater common life out of which associations rise, into which associations bring order, but which associations never completely fulfill. If we reflect, we perceive at once that there is a vast difference between the living together of men which makes a village or city or country on the one hand, and the association of men in a church or trade-union—or even, as we shall see, in a State—on the other. Often state-areas do not even coincide with the areas of effective community, as, for instance, when a subject people, incorporated in an alien State, continues to lead its own manner of life.

The doctrine which makes the State the limit of community and makes all other associations but elements of the State, is contradicted by the whole evolution of the modern State. For the present it will suffice to show that the doctrine, so strangely maintained in the face of history, is contrary to the present fact. Here we are not concerned with what the State ought to be and to include, but with what the State actually is and does include. So regarded, it is quite obvious that the State is neither conterminous nor synonymous with community. Every State has rigid territorial limits, but the modern world, marked off into separate States, is not partitioned into a number of isolated communities. We have already seen that community is a matter of degree, that it is a network of social interrelations here denser, here thinner, whose ever new-woven filaments join men to men across countries and continents. The State, unlike community, is exclusive and determinate. Where one State ends, another begins; where one begins, another ends. No man can owe allegiance to two States, any more than he can serve two masters, but he can enter into the life of as many communities as his sympathies and opportunities will allow.

The State must, therefore, be clearly distinguished from the community which creates it. Community is the common life of beings who are guided essentially from within, actively, spontaneously, and freely (under the conditions prescribed by the laws they make) relating themselves to one another, weaving for themselves the complex web of social unity. But the State works with an instrument which is necessarily formal, prescribing the general external conditions of social life, upholding the main system of those social obligations which may be externally fulfilled. Its instrument resembles, in Aristotle's phrase, no "leaden rule" which can adapt itself to the actual mouldings of the social structure, but an unbending rod which can measure only its general outlines.

It is needless to say that in thus stating the limits of political activity we are not belittling the immeasurable value of that activity. The point is that the State is not equivalent to community, that the political association does not include and can not control the whole life of men. The State is seen to be not community but a peculiarly authoritative association within it. The State is determinate, a closed organization of social life; community is indeterminate, an ever-evolving system spreading beyond and only partially controlled within the definite framework of any State. That framework gives to the portion of the community which it encloses a certain unity and definition, but neither cuts it off from a wider community of which it is essentially part nor within that portion substitutes its own external mode of action, its necessity, for the spontaneity that is the mark of all life, social and other. Social life can no longer in practice and should no longer in theory be summed up in political life. The individual should not be summed up in his citizenship, otherwise the claim of citizenship will itself become a tyranny and its essential moral value be lost. "The modern wilderness of interests" is not to be straightened out into the simple road of citizenship. For the main road of citizenship, which we must make straight as possible, though it intersects a thousand paths of social interest, can not and should not absorb them.

Community, therefore, and not the State, is the "world the spirit has made for itself." "The spirit" does not isolate itself in States, as Hegel's argument assumes. On the contrary, the growth of civilisation means the growth of ever-widening community, the "realisation" of social interest beyond the limits of politically independent groups. Society widens and the sense of community grows.

It is significant to note that MacIver's views have been adopted by Cole as the foundation of the political and

social theory set forth in his version of gild socialism.[23]
Miss Follett, while contending that political reconstruction
must start with the group concept as basic, holds that
neither the individual nor the state can be neglected in the
enthusiasm for pluralism. The problem of the relation
of the individual to the group and of the group to the
state must be considered and solved in any comprehensive
plan of political reform.[24]

7. *The State and Administrative Decentralization*

Finally, in the doctrines of Emile Durkheim one may
note the entry of a capitalistic variety of administrative
syndicalism into the sociological theory of the state.[25] According to his view, the state is adapted only to legislating
with respect to general policies and measures. It is not
competent in the matter of applying these general policies
in varied and specific instances; in other words, it is
ill-fitted for administration, especially in the economic
field. Administrative duties of this nature Durkheim
would hand over to unified and coordinated *syndicates*
of workingmen and employers in each industrial category. Though their economic postulates differ widely, it
is but a short step from Durkheim's theory of the state
to that held by the Gild Socialists.[26] The latter would

[23] Cole, *Social Theory*, pp. 25 ff., 210.
[24] Follett, *The New State*, Introduction, and Pts. I–II.
[25] *Le suicide*, pp. 434 ff.; *De la division du travail social*, ed.
1902, Preface.
[26] Cf. Cole, *Social Theory*, esp. Chaps. V–VIII; also his *Guild
Socialism*. Cole's basic social and political theory is obviously
and admittedly taken from MacIver, *Community: a Sociological
Study*, esp. Chap. II.—For an admirable summary of the various

limit the powers of the state to safeguarding the interests of the citizens as consumers, while they would hand over the control of productive enterprise to greatly modified and strengthened trade-unions. As a general coordinating body they would erect a federal organization—a national commune—representing and linking together the functional associations of society.[27]

8. *Society and the State*

The attitude of the sociologists toward the problem of state activity will be reserved for later discussion. Here, however, it may be pointed out that, in distinction from the advocates of a constructive view of the functions of the state, such as Ward, Giddings, Hobhouse and Stein, there are eminent sociologists who have vigorously championed the view of the state as the "collective policeman" in a form nearly as extreme as that of the classical economists and the statesmen of the Manchester School. Most notable in this group have been Spencer, Novicow, Le Bon and Sumner.

Though there are real and significant differences of opinion among sociological writers as to the nature and importance of the state, there is almost unanimous agreement among them in regard to one fundamental problem, namely, the relation between society and the state. With a few exceptions, like that of Fouillée, sociologists are

pluralistic theories of the state, cf. Coker, "The Technique of the Pluralistic State," in *American Political Science Review*, Vol. XV, pp. 185–213.

[27] For the best history and analysis of gild socialism, cf. Carpenter, *Guild Socialism*.

agreed that society is the more general and basic fact and term which refers to and embraces all forms of associated life, whether that life be among animals or men. The state is a specific association, and is perhaps the most important of several fundamental types of organs or agencies utilized by society to insure that collective life shall be more safe, efficient, and progressive. Though its roots extend far back into the early history of mankind, the state of modern political terminology is a comparatively recent product of social evolution, and by its very origin, as well as by an analysis of its nature, it is demonstrated to be a creation and creature of society. This is the basic point of departure for the sociological analysis of political problems and constitutes the permanent and distinctive contribution of sociology to the theory of the origin and nature of the state.[28]

[28] While not in agreement with the author in all matters of detail, I know of no better brief exposition of this point than MacIver's above-mentioned work, esp. Bk. I, and App. A.

CHAPTER IV

SOCIOLOGICAL CONTRIBUTIONS TO THE STUDY OF THE ORIGINS AND DEVELOPMENT OF THE STATE

1. *The Sociological Analysis of the Foundations of Political Obedience*

A complete sociological theory of the origin of the state entails a consideration of the following problems: the socio-psychological origins of human association in the most general terms; the social and psychic forces involved in the origins of political leadership; the nature and progress of tribal society; the causes and nature of the rise of the territorial state; and the great social stages in the evolution of the state.

The sociological doctrines that have been adduced to explain the origins of human association are numerous and varied; but they are rarely contradictory, and the final synthesis of sociological theory will in all probability accord, in a different degree, recognition to all of them. Here, it will suffice to mention some of the more important views of the better known sociologists. In such a category belong the theories of sympathy from Adam Smith to Sutherland and Giddings; the closely allied doctrine of mutual aid and spontaneous cooperation set forth by such writers as Kropotkin, Novicow and Wallas; the notion of a gregarious instinct as elaborated by McDougall and Trotter; Giddings' emphasis on the "consciousness of kind"; the effect of imitation expounded by Hume, Bagehot, Tarde, Ross and Baldwin; the subordination of the individual by the impressive force of the group as viewed by Durkheim, Le Bon, Sighele, Gumplowicz, Trotter and Sumner; and John Fiske's theory of the prolongation of human infancy.[1]

The socio-psychological explanations of the rise of political superiority and subordination are closely related to these interpetations of the origins of associated life. We have Spencer's doctrine of fear; Bagehot's, Baldwin's and Tarde's theory of imitation; De Greef's and Fouillée's modified version of a theory of political origins through self-interest and a voluntary contract; Novicow's stressing of the rise of exchange and cooperative activity; Durkheim's and Le Bon's insistence upon the influence of social impression; Mallock's, Faguet's and Mumford's exposition of the significance of leadership and dominating personalities; McDougall's theory of an instinct of self-abasement and an emotion of subjection; and the attempt to reach a synthetic interpretation in Giddings' notion of differential response to stimulation and the theory of protocracy, and in the well-balanced studies of Baldwin, Cooley, and Ellwood.[2]

[1] On these points cf. Davis, *Psychological Interpretations of Society;* also my articles in *American Journal of Sociology,* Vols. XXVII–XXVIII; *Sociological Review,* Vols. XIII–XV; *Philosophical Review,* Vol. XXVIII, pp. 248–79; *Political Science Quarterly,* Vol. XXXV, pp. 236–54; *American Journal of Psychology,* Vol. XXXI, pp. 333–69.

[2] For a more detailed analysis of these psychological factors in the state, cf. below, pp. 73–76, 196–206.

2. *Historical Origins of the State*

The first modern attempt to trace the development of political origins from the period of tribal society rested on the theory which was supposed to be of divine origin and sanction and had been confirmed by the generalizations of Aristotle, Bodin, Pufendorf, Locke and Blackstone, namely, that the patriarchal organization of society had been the earliest form of family, social, and political life. This thesis received its ablest synthesis and defense in the *Ancient Law* and other monumental contributions to historical jurisprudence and politics from the pen of Henry Sumner Maine.

This point of view was attacked by J. J. Bachofen in his *Das Mutterrecht,* published in 1860. He maintained the existence of a primordial promiscuity in sexual relations and a subsequent development of a matriarchate or a polity dominated by females. But he was a follower of the methods of Vico and Wolf rather than of Spencer and Morgan, for he based his generalizations upon data drawn from a study of classical mythology and tradition.

This rather archaic methodology was soon abandoned for what has come to be known as the "evolutionary" approach to historical sociology. A group of distinguished scholars, most notable among them being Sir John Lubbock, J. F. McLennan, Herbert Spencer, Albert H. Post, Julius Lippert, Edward B. Tylor, Lewis H. Morgan, Andrew Lang, W. Robertson Smith, James G. Frazer, Charles Letourneau and Daniel G. Brinton, brought the evolutionary principles of Darwinian biology to bear upon the reconstruction of the early history of human society and reached results equally disruptive of the position of Maine.[3] While there were important differences of opinion in matters of detail among these writers, they were in general agreement upon essentials of method and results, and their general doctrine may be summarized as follows: There is an organic law of development in social institutions. One may assume as a major premise a unilateral evolutionary development of institutions, implying gradual and orderly changes, largely the same the world over, and normally proceeding from simple and confused arrangements and relations to complex and well-coordinated adjustments. There is a real psychic unity in mankind, in that the organization and activity of the human mind, as far as its organic constitution and its reactions are concerned, is everywhere generally the same. There is a very considerable similarity of typical geographical environments in different parts of the world, and geographical environment is the main external stimulus to the human mind. This psychic unity of mankind and similarities of geographic environment inevitably give rise to parallelisms and similarities in culture among peoples widely separated in space. In reconstructing the development of human society, therefore, it is permissible to link together a series of isolated examples of any type of culture, taken from the most diverse regions and irrespective of the cultural setting from which the type or example is extracted, in a prearranged and *à priori* scheme of institutional progress, and, at the same time, to

[3] This literature is well summarized, though with no great critical acumen, in Howard, *History of Matrimonial Institutions,* Vol I; and Posada. *Théories modernes sur les origines de la famille, de la société et de l'état.*

hold that this establishes or substantiates the particular assumed scheme of evolutionary development.[4]

Applying these methods and assumptions to the study of early society, these writers arrived at a series of definite conclusions. The monogamous family shows a slow but distinct development from original promiscuity, and the family of any type is a late product developing within the older kinship or gentile organization of society. In the history of gentile society certain definite and successive stages can be isolated and their sequence correlated with the development of material culture. The first type of extensive human grouping was found in the endogamous horde, where there was neither fixed family nor other wider relations. This stage was followed by the appearance of definite kinship or gentile society associated with the exogamous clan, which was inseparably connected with a totemic complex.[5] The earliest form of gentile society was the maternal clan, which was in time invariably succeeded by the paternal gens, this transformation in the basis of relationships being definitely correlated with progressive advances in material culture. The paternal gens was gradually solidified into a patriarchal organization of society, which, through the development of property and the infiltration of foreigners from economic attraction, was in time superseded, through the abolition of kinship principles, by the establishment of the territorial state and civil society. This orderly synthesis of

[4] For a frank statement, or better, confession, of the classical method of anthropological reconstruction, cf. Spencer, *Autobiography,* Vol. II, pp. 325 ff. Some members of this school, particularly E. B. Tylor, were more critical than Spencer.

[5] It should be pointed out that Frazer, in his *Totemism and Exogamy,* has admitted that the two are not inseparable.

social and political evolution was most comprehensively organized and most effectively set forth in the famous work on *Ancient Society* by Lewis H. Morgan.[6]

Since Morgan's day new methods of anthropological investigation and synthesis and more thorough studies of existing primitive societies have served largely to discredit the principles of investigation followed by the evolutionary or classical school of anthropologists and to disprove the conclusions which they reached. In fact, more careful investigation according to the old methods enabled Westermarck to prove inaccurate the assumption of a primitive promiscuity.[7] The basis for the newer point of view was laid by very painstaking studies of primitive cultural areas and an attempt to study the data in an objective manner. Space forbids the enumeration of more than a few examples of this type of indispensable anthropological research, but as representative of it may be cited the studies of Australian data by Cunow, Brown and Thomas; Rivers' great monographs on the *Todas* and the *History of Melanesian Society;* Seligmann's survey of the Veddas; the Torres Straits investigations undertaken by a group of English scholars; the investigation of African data by Roscoe and Pechuel-Loesche; and particularly the careful studies of American areas by the participants in the Jesup North Pacific Expedition, and of other American areas by Boas, Wissler, Lowie, Kroeber, Goldenweiser, Spinden, Dixon, Parker, Goddard, Mooney, Speck, Swanton and others.

[6] For a more critical and discriminating view, cf. Tylor, "On a Method of Investigating the Development of Institutions," in *Journal of the Anthropological Institute,* Vol. XVIII, pp. 245-72.

[7] *History of Human Marriage,* 1891.

This unequalled body of data, together with a more objective and scientific attitude toward its interpretation, has not only produced more reliable doctrines concerning social evolution, but has also shown that the facts of social development are quite different from what was earlier supposed. The more critical school has proved that the assumption of a universal law of evolution from the simple to the complex is not invariably true with respect to cultural or social institutions. It has shown that parallelisms in culture and social organization in different areas do not imply identical antecedents or necessarily bring about similar subsequent developments. Similarities may grow out of "cultural convergencies" proceeding from widely varied antecedents, or they may be produced by imitation of a common pattern.[8]

The application of this more scientific method to the study of primitive society has been nothing short of revolutionary. The universality of gentile society cannot be proved; many groups have developed to a relatively high stage of culture without any system of relationship wider than the family. Where gentile society exists there is no general tendency for relationships to change from a maternal to a paternal basis; in fact, it may be doubted if there is one well-authenticated example of an independent change in kinship from maternal to paternal in the whole range of assured data bearing upon primitive society.

[8] Excellent discussions of the newer anthropological methodology are to be found in Boas, *Mind of Primitive Man*, Chaps. IV–VII; Lowie, *Culture and Ethnology;* Goldenweiser, "Principle of Limited Possibilities in the Development of Culture," in *Journal of American Folklore,* Vol. XXVI, pp. 259 ff.; and "Four Phases of Anthropological Thought," in *Publications of the American Sociological Society,* Vol. XVI, pp. 50–69.

Further, there is no evidence that maternal kinship is correlated with lower material culture or paternal kinship with more advanced culture. Finally, totemism has been entirely dissociated from exogamy. It is evident that the whole fabric of the scheme of social evolution provided by the evolutionary group has perished, and Lowie has well expressed the obituary notice of this school.[9]

To sum up. There is no fixed succession of maternal and paternal descent; sibless tribes may pass directly into the matrilineal or the patrilineal condition; if the highest civilisations emphasize the paternal side of the family, so do many of the lowest; and the social history of any particular people cannot be reconstructed from any generally valid scheme of social evolution but only in the light of its known and probable cultural relations with neighboring peoples.

These more critical principles and more assured results in anthropological research have been chiefly an American product, associated with the work of Franz Boas and his pupils.[10]

It is not to be assumed, of course, that all sociologists have assimilated the results of the more critical ethnology; indeed, most of them rest their theories of social evolution on the old Morganian ethnology, and not a few regard the work of Boas and the critical school as impious if not impish. But they cannot long disregard these epoch-

[9] *Primitive Society,* p. 185.

[10] Excellent syntheses of the newer views of primitive societies are contained in the notable works of Marett, *Anthropology;* Lowie, *Primitive Society;* Wissler, *Man and Culture;* and Goldenweiser, *Early Civilization.* Another remarkable synthesis of American data is to be found in Wissler, *The American Indian.*

making advances, and it may safely be predicted that at no distant date the sociological theory of political origins will rest upon the firm foundation of critical ethnology.[11]

3. *The Sociological Theory of the Development of the State*

The next problem in the sociological theory of political origins concerns the tracing of the rise of the developed territorial state.   Older views, following Aristotle, traced it as a natural expansion of the groupings of tribal society. Morgan and the evolutionary school accounted for political origins on the basis of the rise of property and the necessity of a more advanced type of political and legal institutions to cope with the more complex economic problems resulting therefrom.   Gradually, however, the doctrine has gained ground that the territorial state was primarily the product of forcible subjugation through long continued warfare among primitive groups.   Today this may be said to be *the* sociological theory of political origins and development.   This view is not a new one; it certainly may be traced back as far as Polybius and has had its exponents in every succeeding age.[12]   Hume in his

[11] Almost the only frank recognitions by sociologists of the implications of the newer anthropology known to the writer are to be found in Ellwood's excellent article on "Theories of Cultural Evolution," in *American Journal of Sociology,* Vol. XXIII, pp. 779–800; and Ogburn's paper on "The Historical Method in the Analysis of Social Phenomena," in *Publications of the American Sociological Society,* Vol. XVI, pp. 70–83.

[12] I have tried to summarize briefly the history of this view of political origins, including the theory of Gumplowicz and later writers, in an article in the *Journal of Race Development,* Vol. IX, pp. 394–419. Cf. also Bristol, *Social Adaptation,* pp. 162 ff.

Essays and Ferguson in his *History of Civil Society* may be regarded as the real founders of the modern version of this doctrine, while Spencer and Bagehot worked it over in the light of evolutionary concepts; but it is with the work of Ludwig Gumplowicz and his theory of the "race struggle" that this important contribution to the sociological theory of the state is usually associated. Gumplowicz forecast this interpretation in his brochure on *Rasse und Staat* (1875) and expanded it in two later works, *Der Rassenkampf* (1883) and *Grundriss der Soziologie* (1885). It has been taken up and elaborated, among others, by Ratzenhofer in Austria, Oppenheimer and Simmel in Germany, Jenks in England, and Small and Ward in America.

Briefly stated, this theory rests upon a doctrine of group constitution of society, based on the principle of *syngenism* or "the phenomenon which consists in the fact that invariably in associated modes of life, definite groups of men, feeling themselves closely bound together by common interests, endeavor to function as a single element in the struggle for domination." From the earliest days the "process of history" has consisted chiefly in the struggle between social groups for the advancement of their economic interests. The conquest of one group by another led to the subjection of the conquered and the ascendency of the conquerors, who gradually but continuously increased the territorial scope of their authority. In order to gain internal strength and unity, however, the rulers of the expanding groups were compelled to grant concessions to the conquered, and with this the process of cultural assimilation began, physical amalgamation was gradually achieved, and the national state was produced. During this process social classes, religious and economic, were developed within the state in the shape of conquerors and conquered; and as political institutions developed, these classes struggled for political power, each seeking to secure and .use the law-making authority in its own interest. From these crude origins this conflict of interest-groups within the state has furnished the raw material and the *rationale* of political processes.

Though this interpretation of political development has received the general assent of sociologists,[13] it has been vigorously criticized as minimizing the element of cooperation and other peaceful agencies which have undoubtedly been a potent factor in the history of the state. Among the better known writers who have expressed such views are Sutherland in his *Origin and Growth of the Moral Instinct;* Kropotkin in his *Mutual Aid: a Factor in Evolution;* and Novicow in his *La critique du Darwinism social,* and *The Mechanism and Limits of Human Association.*[14] Eclectic writers have tried to work out a synthesis designed to show that, while conflict has played the greater part in political origins, peaceful and cooperative elements have not been without great influence in the past and will probably be even more significant in the future. Such a point of view has characterized the doctrine of Giddings, Hayes, Stein and Tarde.[15] Novicow,

[13] Cf. Ward, *Pure Sociology,* pp. 204 ff.; *American Journal of Sociology,* Vol. VII, p. 762; Vol. XV, pp. 679–80; *Publications of the American Economic Association,* third series, Vol. V, No. 2, pp. 187 ff.

[14] Cf. *Journal of International Relations,* Vol. XII, pp. 238–65.

[15] Giddings, *Principles of Sociology,* p. 316; Hayes, *Introduction to the Study of Sociology,* pp. 538 ff.; Stein, *La question*

Commons, Oppenheimer, and Loria have analyzed the economic factors which have figured significantly in the origins of the state, whether in war or in peace.

4. *Stages of Political Development*

There remains to be considered as a part of the sociological theory of political origins, the various illuminating attempts which have been made by sociologists to classify the stages of political development. Comte related political progress to his famous three stages of history, the theological-military, the metaphysical-legal and the positive-industrial.[16] Spencer conceived of political progress as consisting in the advance from a military to an industrial state and in the possible future transition to an ethical state.[17] Bagehot traced political development through the periods of the cementing of custom, the conflict of customs and the origin of states, to the age of free discussion and parliamentary government.[18] Durkheim has viewed the process as a change from mechanical and repressive solidarity in society to organic and functional solidarity.[19] De Greef has traced political evolution from a state of despotic authority to one of voluntary contract.[20] Ratzenhofer and Small have looked upon political progress as chiefly a change from a "conquest-state" to a "culture-

sociale, pp. 123–4, 352 ff., 450 ff.; Tarde, *Les transformations du pouvoir*, pp. 36, 50, 174–85.

[16] *Principles of a Positive Polity*, Vol. III, pp. 91 ff.

[17] *Principles of Sociology*, Vol. II, pp. 603 ff.

[18] *Physics and Politics*, passim.

[19] *De la division du travail social*, passim.

[20] *Introduction à la sociologie;* and *La structure générale des sociétés*.

state." [21]   Oppenheimer has classified political progress
under the headings of primitive feudal states, maritime
states, developed feudal states, and constitutional states.[22]
Hobhouse has held that political development can best be
interpreted by viewing it as a change of the dominant
principle of political life from kinship to authority and
from authority to citizenship.[23]   Again, there are Giddings' well-known divisions of social and political evolution, representing a synthesis of the classifications of
Comte, Bagehot and Spencer, the military-religious, the
liberal-legal and the economic-ethical.[24]   Finally, one may
note Wundt's synthetic socio-psychological classification
of social, political and cultural genesis.   He finds four
main stages of development, that of primitive men of the
earliest cultural ages; that of totemism, or the era of
kinship grouping or gentile society; that of the heroes and
gods, in which develops the idea of deity, leadership, property, the state, individuality and social classes; and that
of humanity, accompanied by the growth of large political
entities and the development of the sentiment of human
solidarity and brotherhood.[25]   All of these schemes of
political evolution possess the common virtue of correlating political progress with some causal factor or situation
in the social environment.

[21] Small, *General Sociology,* pp. 190 ff.
[22] *The State,* passim.
[23] *Morals in Evolution,* Vol. I, pp. 42 ff.; *Social Evolution and Political Theory,* pp. 128 ff.
[24] *Principles of Sociology,* Bk. III, Chap. IV.
[25] Wundt, *Elements of Folk Psychology, passim.*

CHAPTER V

1. *Demography and Population Analysis*

Political scientists have for a long time been agreed
that any catalog of the essential elements of the state
must include population, territory, and sovereign power.
Aside from elaborate metaphysical studies of the latter, however, they have given little attention to a fundamental analysis of these basic elements in political life,
though in this way alone is it possible to penetrate beyond the superficial externalities of political processes.

The contributions of sociology to the description and
analysis of the social population have been diverse and
epoch-making, and must be differentiated even for brief
summarization. First in volume, if not in ultimate importance, should be placed those indispensable studies of
population conditions which are usually grouped under the
branch of descriptive sociology known as demography.
In modern times this work has been done mainly by public authorities and expert advisers in connection with the
official census. It is concerned chiefly with the gathering
of descriptive data which furnish the basis of such important information as relates to birth-rates and death-
rates, age-classes, industrial groups, distribution of wealth,

distribution of population between country and city, ethnic
composition, vitality classes, etc., and, by comparison of
data gathered at different periods, to the dynamic aspects
of these problems indicated by changes in the population
and its characteristics. The collection and interpretation
of this material, which is absolutely indispensable to any
scientific or effective statesmanship, has been the work of
a large number of industrious scholars, among whom may
be named Schmoller, Meitzen, Lexis and Hansen in Germany; Dumont, Levasseur and Leroy-Beaulieu in France;
Nitti in Italy; Newsholme, Welton and Bowley in England; and Willcox, Mayo-Smith, Wright, Durand and
Bailey in the United States.[1] An integral part of this
field, though utilized chiefly for the study of the depressed
or laboring classes in industrial cities, is the social survey—a technique devised by Frédéric Le Play and brought
to public attention by the famous investigations of Booth
and Rowntree in London and York. It has been subse-
quently employed with great success in Europe and America, and from this line of investigation has come most of
our knowledge concerning the living conditions among
the urban proletariat—data upon which much of the remedial legislation relative to labor conditions must be
based.[2]

[1] Notable works along this line are: Hansen, *Die drei Bevölkerungsstufen;* the annals and monographs edited by Gustav
Schmoller; Levasseur, *La population francaise;* Nitti, *Population
and the Social System;* Bowley, *Wages in the United Kingdom;* Newsholme, *Elements of Vital Statistics;* Wright, *Practical Sociology;* Mayo-Smith, *Statistics and Sociology;* Bailey,
Modern Social Conditions; Fairchild, *Immigration;* Jenks and
Lauck, *The Immigration Problem.*

[2] Cf. Ellwood, "The Le Play Method of Social Investigation,"
in *American Journal of Sociology*, Vol. II, pp. 662 ff.—Kellogg,

It has been especially in this field of demography that there has developed one of the most important of the sociological techniques, namely, social statistics. Having actually originated with Bodin and with certain mathematicians and scientists of the seventeenth century, the science of statistics is nevertheless conventionally dated from the work of Adolphe Quetelet, a Belgian contemporary of Comte. While it has rather definite limitations in application to social problems, there can be no doubt that the statistical technique is the only one which can elevate sociology and political science to the level of quantitative sciences. By its assistance alone can the necessary data be assembled, sifted and arranged in order to furnish the basis for sociological generalizations or political theorizing which may possess some degree of assured validity.[3]

Closely related to this field of sociological investigation is physical anthropology as applied to modern social and political problems. It was long popular, following Gobineau and others, to base the interpretation of the political life and organization of various modern states upon their alleged racial composition and the supposed psychic traits which flowed therefrom. This confession of analytical bankruptcy has not yet entirely disappeared from contem-

The Pittsburgh Survey (six vols.) sets forth what was probably the most notable achievement in this field in the United States. The literature of this subject is well summarized by Small in *Encyclopedia Americana*, Vol. XXV, p. 215.

[3] Cf. Hankins, *Adolphe Quetelet as Statistician;* Westergaard, "The Scope and Method of Statistics," in *Quarterly Publications of the American Statistical Association,* Vol. XV, pp. 225–91; (also Vol. XIV, pp. 1-121) ; Merz, *History of European Thought in the Nineteenth Century,* Vol. II. Chap. XII; Wallas, *Human Nature in Politics,* Chaps. IV-V; Koren (editor), *A History of Statistics.*

porary political theory.[4]   A vulgar fallacy, not wholly
absent in Aristotelian doctrine, it may be traced back at
least as far as Romanticism and the reaction against the
French Revolution.   Here there developed those misleading dogmas of the fickleness and political incompetence
of the French as contrasted with the unparalleled political
sagacity and capacity for achievement of the Teutonic
and Anglo-Saxon peoples.   It was further reinforced by
the amusing but tragic combination of fallacies in Gobineau's *Essay on the Inequality of the Human Races,* with
its eulogy of the Aryan race, was solemnly confirmed by
the philologists, and reached its *reductio ad absurdum* in
the dithyrambic exultation of H. S. Chamberlain [5] over
the cultural supremacy of the Teuton.   Even modern biology was drawn upon to support the doctrine of racial
superiority, and Francis Galton came forward with his
allegation of the vast psycho-physical superiority of the
"mythical Greek" over the average member of the intellectual classes of the present day.   It was left for sociological historians such as Fustel de Coulanges and Frederick Seebohm to challenge the Romanticist-Teutonic philosophy of history, for W. Z. Ripley and Giuseppe Sergi
to shatter forever the myth of an Aryan race and to show
the hopeless confusion and mixture of races in every
leading European state,[6] and for Franz Boas to demon-
strate that no sufficient evidence can at present be adduced

[4] Cf. Demolins, *Anglo-Saxon Superiority,* recently utilized
by McDougall in his *Group Mind,* pp. 275 ff.; Grant, *The
Passing of the Great Race;* Stoddard, *The Rising Tide of Color;*
also Corbin, *The Return of the Middle Class.*

[5] *The Foundations of the Nineteenth Century.* Cf. also Burr,
America's Race Heritage; and Gould, *America; A Family Matter.*

[6] Ripley, *The Races of Europe;* Sergi, *The Mediterranean Race.*

to prove the biological superiority of any race or sub-race.[7] By the results of these studies the racial interpretation of politics has been utterly discredited and can in the future be the refuge alone •of the uninformed or the advocate.[8]

As penetrating more deeply into the biological foundations of the social population may be mentioned those studies which are associated with the names of Galton, Pearson, Bateson and Carr-Saunders in England; of Ammon and Schallmayer in Germany; of Vacher de Lapouge and Jacoby in France; and of Tenney, Conklin, Davenport, Keller and Holmes in the United States.[9] The investigations of these writers have brought under scientific consideration such vital questions as the application of biological data to society, not through the vagaries of the organic analogy, but through the study of man as a member of the animal kingdom; the nature of the biological classes in human society; the problem of whether man as an animal is improving or deteriorating; the pos-

[7] *The Mind of Primitive Man,* Chap. I.

[8] The whole subject of racial differences is critically surveyed by Hankins in his forthcoming work, *The Racial Basis of Civilization.*

[9] Galton, *Natural Inheritance;* and *Inquiries into the Human Faculty and its Development;* Pearson, *National Life from the Standpoint of Science;* Bateson, *Biological Fact and the Structure of Society;* Carr-Saunders, *The Problem of Population;* de Lapouge, *Les sélections sociales;* Jacoby, *Etudes sur la sélection;* Ammon, *Die Gesellschaftsordnung und ihre natürlichen Grundlagen;* Schallmayer, *Vererbung und Auslese im Lebenslauf der Völker;* Tenney, *Social Democracy and Population;* Davenport, *Heredity in its Relation to Eugenics;* Conklin, "Biology and Democracy," *Scribners,* Vol. 65, pp. 403–12; and *The Direction of Human Evolution;* Keller, *Societal Evolution;* Holmes, *The Trend of the Race.*

sibility of introducing artificial selection in human society
by a scientific scheme of eugenics; the results of racial
mixture and isolation; the problem of whether modern
biology lends its support to aristocracy or democracy in
politics and social organization; and the relation of these
biological problems to sound statesmanship. While there
is by no means as yet entire agreement among these writers, it is certain that the results of their researches have
been sufficiently significant and assured to merit the most
careful scrutiny of the statesman.

The "differential" biology of the above writers has
been accompanied by the cultivation of differential psychology and the study of individual and class differences
in the psychic realm. The results of this line of investigation have been appropriated for sociology by several writers, most notably by Giddings in his famous "Provisional
Distribution of the Population of the United States into
Psychological Classes"—ideo-motor, ideo-emotional, dog-
matic-emotional and critical-intellectual.[10] Wallas, while
not risking a classification of his own, has argued for a
careful statistical study of the psychological characteristics of the different classes in the social population.[11]
F. H. Hankins is now engaged in an attempt at a synthesis of differential biology and psychology with particular reference to the problem of the assumptions and
policies of modern democracy.[12]

[10] *Psychological Review*, Vol. VIII. pp. 337-49; cf, also *Inductive Sociology*, pp. 84 ff.
[11] *Human Nature in Politics*, pp. 123 ff., 132 ff.; also *Our
Social Heritage*, Chap. IV.
[12] See his article in the *Political Science Quarterly*, Vol.
XXXVIII, pp. 388-412; also his paper in the *Publications of the
American Sociological Society*, Vol. XVII, pp. 27-39.

In concluding these contributions of sociologists to a more thorough analysis of the social population, one must note the sociological synthesis wrought out in a treatment such as that of Giddings in the chapter on "The Social Population" in his *Principles of Sociology.*[13] Here are brought under review the psycho-physical factors involved in the genesis and functioning of any permanent population. Beginning with the geographical and biological forces and elements related to the aggregation, congregation and perpetuation of a population in any region, he carries his analysis on to a consideration of the process of socialization, the genesis of a society and the evolution of social classes and interests. In his more recent works he has suggested an interesting classification of the social population in its relation to political authority. All who dwell within the limits of a state he designates as subjects of authority. The loyal subjects, who participate in the common activities of the citizens, are members of the state, and these may be further subdivided into makers of moral authority, makers of legal authority, and agents of legal authority. The makers of moral authority include all those who in any way influence public opinion; the makers of legal authority are those who exercise the right of suffrage and elect the law-makers; the agents of legal authority are the authorized representatives of the makers of legal authority, i. e., the government.[14]

Equally significant is the procedure outlined by Gumplowicz and worked out in detail by Ratzenhofer and Small, namely, the study and analysis of the social popula-

[13] Op. cit., Bk. II, Chap. I.
[14] Giddings, *Elements of Sociology,* pp. 201-2; and *Inductive Sociology,* p. 211.

tion as a complex of differentiated and functional organizations for the realization of a definite set of vital human interests which determine the range and type of social groupings, aspirations and activities.[15] In short, one may safely say that such studies as have been briefly catalogued have changed the category of "population" from what has been in the hands of conventional political scientists a vague, meaningless and metaphysical entity into a vital living reality, a knowledge of which is indispensable to any adequate treatment of theoretical politics or to the pursuit of any valid policy in practical statesmanship.

2. *Geographical Factors in Politics*

Not less important have been the contributions of sociological students who have centered their attention upon a scientific study of the geographical environments of political societies. The beginnings of such studies may be traced back to Hippocrates and Aristotle, and they were continued to modern times by Cicero, Vitruvius, Strabo, Vegetius, Aquinas, Bodin and Montesquieu.[16] The progress of geographical discovery with such men as Alexander von Humboldt, along with the development of modern natural science, enabled Karl Ritter at the opening of the nineteenth century to found the science of anthropogeog-

[15] Small, *General Sociology,* pp. 196 ff.
[16] Cf. the brief review in the article on "The Relation of Geography to History," in the *Journal of Geography,* Vol. XX, pp. 321–37. A very superficial and incomplete history of anthropogeography is provided in Koller, *The Theory of Environment.* Professor Franklin Thomas is now engaged on a systematic survey. See also Ripley, *Political Science Quarterly,* Vol. X.

raphy, which was popularized by a number of his pupils, such as Guyot and Peschel. Working upon the basis of Ritter's contributions, the further progress of discovery, and the promulgation of the Darwinian hypothesis, Friedrich Ratzel was able to systematize the subject a generation ago. Ratzel not only wrought out with thoroughness the science of human geography in general, but also made elaborate applications of the subject to history and politics.[17] Works of a similarly comprehensive sort have been produced by other writers in this field, most notably by Reclus, Brunhes, Vallaux, Vidal de la Blache, and Semple.

In addition to general syntheses such as those of Ratzel and Reclus, other students of anthropogeography have produced valuable treatments of special phases of the subject. Cowan and Mackinder have shown the importance of strategic position and possession of key regions for historical progress and political supremacy.[18] Demolins and Brunhes have traced the importance for history and political organization of the routes which have been followed by the leading peoples in world history.[19] Metchnikoff has indicated the relation of the river basin en-

[17] Ratzel's major works in the field are *Anthropogeographie; Der Staat und sein Boden;* and *Politische Geographie.* His doctrines have appeared in English in a revised version in Semple, *Influences of Geographical Environment,* but the best brief summary of them is to be found in his own statement in Helmolt's *Weltgeschichte* (Vol. I, Chap. III), which is, fortunately, available in English translation.

[18] Cowan, *Master-Clues in World History;* Mackinder, *Democratic Ideals and Reality.*

[19] Demolins, *Comment la route crée le type social;* Brunhes, *Human Geography.* For the United States the subject is discussed in detail in Hulbert, *Historic Highways.*

vironment to the early history of society and the origin of states.[20]   Le Play and Geddes have demonstrated the significance of natural physiographic regions for social, economic and political life and for problems of social and political reconstruction.[21]   Hann and Ward have systematically studied the effect of climate on social and political processes; and Huntington has not only studied climatic influences in their static aspects, but has also postulated a stimulating and original dynamic theory of climatic pulsations, and has indicated the relation between climatic changes, on the one hand, and the decline of historical civilizations and the historic migrations of peoples, on the other.[22]   Dexter has investigated the problem of the relation of barometric pressure and weather conditions to human conduct, and has shown the bearing of weather influences on the frequency of crime and the volume of constructive effort in society.[23]   Brunhes has brought a dynamic point of view into the field; he has studied the changes wrought by man in the physical environment and has held that the artificial environment, such as a city-block, must be regarded as much a part of the physical environment as an adjoining mountain, lake or river.[24]

[20] *La civilisation et les grandes fleuves historiques.*

[21] Geddes, *Cities in Evolution;* Geddes and Branford, *The Coming Polity.*

[22] Hann, *Handbuch der Klimatologie;* Ward, *Climate; Considered Especially in Its Relation to Man;* Huntington, *The Pulse of Asia; Civilization and Climate; World-Power and Evolution;* and *Climatic Changes.*

[23] *Conduct and the Weather;* and *Weather Influences.*

[24] *Human Geography;* Cf. also Brunhes and Vallaux, *La géographie de l'histoire.*

Critical ethnologists, such as Boas, Wissler, Lowie and Goldenweiser, have reminded the students of geography that culture is the dynamic factor and that environment simply imposes the general limitations upon cultural possibilities and furnishes a part of the raw material for the development of civilization.[25]   Finally, Giddings has attempted to work out a theory of social causation which synthesizes the environmental and psychological factors in one comprehensive account of social evolution.[26]   These contributions to the anthropogeographical sociology have now, for the first time, made possible an accurate and scientific realization of Montesquieu's aspiration to describe and analyze those natural conditions which help to produce the social and cultural conditions to which any sound policy or any adequate and appropriate body of laws must conform.

3.   *Economic Elements in the State*

Writers on political theory with a sociological orientation have emphasized the part played by economic factors in political processes.   This, indeed, has been one of the most important phases of the elaboration of the chief sociological thesis in political theory, namely, that social forces are anterior and fundamental to political processes. While the doctrine of the economic determination of pol-

[25] Boas, *The Mind of Primitive Man,* pp. 159–64; Lowie, *Culture and Ethnology,* Chap. III; Goldenweiser, "Culture and Environment," in *American Journal of Sociology,* Vol. XXI, pp. 628–33.   Cf. also Wissler, *Man and Culture.*
[26] "A Theory of Social Causation," in *Publications of the American Economic Association,* third series, Vol. V. No. 2, pp. 139–74; also "Pluralistic Behavior," loc. cit.

itics is regarded by the governing classes in modern *bourgeois* states as somewhat incendiary and scandalous, it is an old and respectable notion which has been common to most of the leading thinkers in the history of political philosophy. Plato contended that private property tended to dominate and corrupt politics, and that there could be no honestly and efficiently conducted state so long as it remained.[27] Aristotle described the economic basis of political classes and parties; analyzed the economic determination of political policies; and set forth the economic causes and remedies of political revolutions.[28] Machiavelli held that the presence of a large number of idle and wealthy citizens was fatal to republican government, that the accumulation of great fortunes must be prevented if the rule of merit in politics was to be hoped for, and particularly warned against the oppression of the laboring classes.[29] Hobbes called attention to the economic basis of political ambition and conflicts.[30] Harrington held that political power invariably followed economic ascendency, and that a stable government could be founded only on equality of possessions.[31] Locke maintained that private property was the cause and chief end of the origin of government, and that revolution was justifiable when the objects of government were defeated.[32] Montesquieu em-

[27] *Republic;* cf. Coker, *Readings in Political Philosophy,* pp. 30-1, 33-4.

[28] *Politics;* cf. Coker, op. cit., pp. 84-8, 100-1.

[29] Cf. Detmold, *Writings of Niccolo Machiavelli,* Vol. II, pp. 210-11, 371, 448-50.

[30] *Leviathan;* and *Philosophical Rudiments concerning Government;* cf. Coker, op. cit., pp. 302 ff.

[31] *Oceana*; cf. Coker, op. cit., pp. 359 ff.

[32] *Two Treatises of Government;* cf. Coker, op. cit., pp. 403 ff.

phasized the part played by industry and commerce in political policies.[33]

John Adams held that economic conditions determined political notions and aspirations, and that the significant political divisions throughout history had been founded upon the opposition between the rich and the poor.[34] Madison stated that the chief cause of political factions was "the various and unequal distribution of property." [35] Jefferson believed that government could retain purity and virtue only when founded upon an agricultural economy.[36] Webster maintained that the protection of property was the chief end of government, that political loyalty could be assured only by giving citizens an economic stake in politics, and that the property qualification for voting should be retained in certain cases.[37] The most complete statement of the economic determination of political activity by an early American writer was contributed by Calhoun, and he frankly proposed to recognize this fact in the reconstruction of representative government.[38] Lincoln expressed his belief in the economic determination of political action, stated that "labor is the superior of capital and deserves much the higher consideration," and contended that the international class consciousness of the laborer should be the strongest hu-

[33] *The Spirit of Laws*, Bks. XX, XXI, XXVI.

[34] *Life and Works of John Adams*, Vol. VI, pp. 530-1.

[35] *The Federalist*, No. X.

[36] *Works of Jefferson*, Ford ed., Vol III, pp. 268-9; Vol. IV, p. 479.

[37] *The Writings and Speeches of Daniel Webster*, National ed., Vol. I, pp. 214-5; Vol. V, pp. 13 ff.

[38] *The Works of J. C. Calhoun*, Vol. I, pp. 15-16, 24-5; Vol. II, pp. 631-2.

man bond next to the family affection.[39] With the Ricardian Socialists, Thompson, Gray, Hodgskin and Bray, and with Karl Marx, the doctrine of the economic determination of political institutions, as also of other social institutions, became one of the foremost dogmas of social and economic science.[40]

Sociologists have from the first recognized the importance of the economic factor in politics. Comte, Spencer and Giddings have contended that modern society and government have been reshaped by the economic changes since the Industrial Revolution, and have based their classification of the stages of social and political evolution upon a recognition of this fact.[41] The most significant of the sociological contributions along this line has been associated with the doctrine that society is a complex of conflicting interest-groups, the struggles of which are adjusted by the state. This notion, elaborated by Gumplowicz, Oppenheimer, Ratzenhofer, Small, Bentley, Loria and others, lays a broad foundation for the doctrine of the determining influence of economic factors as the chief dynamic element in the conflict of interests in modern society.

While all of the writers of this group have made a liberal allowance for the operation of economic factors, Gumplowicz, Oppenheimer and Loria have accepted a thoroughgoing doctrine of economic determinism in political processes.[42] Oppenheimer's work is the most logical

[39] *Works of Abraham Lincoln,* Nicolai and Hay, Vol. I, pp. 11, 613; Vol. II, pp. 105, 503.

[40] Cf. Lowenthal, *The Ricardian Socialists;* and Seligman, *The Economic Interpretation of History.*

[41] Cf. above, pp. 55–6, and below, pp. 169–73.

[42] Cf. above, pp. 52–5, and below, pp. 101–5, 146–7.

and consistent exposition of this important thesis. He holds that there have been two modes of obtaining the means of subsistence throughout history—work and robbery. Work and the exchange of products he designates as the *economic means;* robbery, or the appropriation of the result of the work of others, as the *political means.* History has been primarily a record of the struggle of the one against the other. Thus far the political means has been triumphant, but there is every evidence that the economic means is about to become ascendent and exterminate the political means. With its victory the state, the developed political means, will be replaced by society, the developed economic means. In this way the dogmas of Marx and Gumplowicz, with a considerable admixture of Henry George, are blended into a logical and, to some, convincing philosophy of history and politics:[43]

I propose in the following discussion to call one's own labor and the equivalent exchange of one's own labor for the labor of others, the "economic means" for the satisfaction of needs, while the unrequited appropriation of the labor of others will be called the "political means." . . .

All world history, from primitive times up to our own civilization, presents a single phase, a contest, namely, between the economic and the political means; and it can present only this phase until we have achieved free citizenship.

The state is an organization of the political means. No state, therefore, can come into being until the economic means has created a definite number of objects for the satisfaction of needs, which objects may be taken away or appropriated by war-like robbery.

Libraries full of books have been written on the delimitation of the concepts "state" and "society." The problem,

[43] Oppenheimer, *The State,* passim.

however, from our point of view has an easy solution. The "state" is the fully developed political means, "society" the fully developed economic means. Heretofore state and society were indissolubly intertwined; in the "free-men's citizenship," there will be no "state" but only "society." [44]

Loria and Commons have made important contribu-ions to the economic basis of political sovereignty which are analyzed in a later chapter dealing with the sociologi-cal theories of sovereignty.[45] Novicow, in the effort to combat pseudo-Darwinian sociology with its glorification of war, has perhaps exaggerated the influence of trade, commerce and exchange on political institutions. He be-lieves that commerce was the all-sufficient cause of the origin of states and the chief factor in political evolution. With the development of world commerce we may soon ex-pect the appearance of the world state.[46] Brooks, Ross and Myers have set forth with vigor and courage the achievements of the representatives of great wealth in capturing American political life and building up the con-trol of the plutocracy which has not yet been even par-tially dislodged.[47] Such descriptive studies are, to many, nore convincing than dogmatic theorizing as to the effect of economics on politics. The detailed analysis of the

[44] Ibid., pp. 25, 27, 275–6.

[45] Cf. below, pp. 126–39.

[46] Novicow, *La critique du Darwinism social;* and "The Mechanism and Limits of Human Association" in *American Journal of Sociology,* Vol. XXIII, pp. 289–349.

[47] Brooks, *Corruption in American Politics and Life;* Ross, *Sin and Society;* and *The Social Trend;* Weyl, *The New Democ-racy;* Myers, *History of Great American Fortunes.*

methods whereby economic factors have gained ascendency in modern society through the activity of the representatives of capitalism has been the work of Veblen in America, Hobson and Webb in England, and Sombart in Germany.[48] The case for modern capitalism has been vigorously stated by Withers, Eddy, Walker and Day.[49]

4. *Psychological Influences in Political Processes*

Among the most promising and flourishing of the various contributions of sociology to political theory has been the discussion of the psychological factors in social processes which react upon the state and political institutions. This line of approach, like the classification of economic factors in the state, is not a novel or original product of recent sociological thought. It was distinctly anticipated by Aristotle, the Stoics and Epicureans, as well as by Machiavelli, Hobbes, Spinoza, Locke, Hume and Adam Smith. Many of these earlier contributions were appropriated by Comte, who also is notable for his systematization of a psychological theory of historical and

[48] Veblen, *The Theory of the Leisure Class; The Theory of Business Enterprise; The Vested Interests and the State of the Industrial Arts;* and *The Engineers and the Price System;* Hobson, *Evolution of Modern Capitalism;* and *Work and Wealth;* Sombart, *Der moderne Kapitalismus;* and *The Quintessence of Capitalism.*—The ablest appreciation by a political scientist of the economic factor in politics is to be found in Beard, *The Economic Basis of Politics.* An able critique of the doctrine of economic determinism is to be found in Lippmann, *Public Opinion,* Pt. IV.

[49] Withers, *The Case for Capitalism;* Eddy, *Property;* Walker, *The Things that are Cæsar's;* Day, *The Raid on Prosperity;* and *My Neighbor the Working-Man.*

political progress and for an elaboration of the thesis of the socio-psychic solidarity of mankind.[50]

In briefly cataloguing the development of the analysis of psychological factors in society and the state, it will perhaps be useful to divide the writers into two chief groups—those who stress non-intellectual factors, and those who emphasize rational or intellectualistic elements. Some overlapping is unavoidable, for some writers have developed more than one line of psychological analysis. Tarde, Baldwin and Ross have analyzed the influence of imitation and repetition in social and political processes.[51] Durkheim, Le Bon, Sumner, Sighele, Trotter and Gumplowicz have made clear the manner in which the group mind dominates and coerces the individual mind.[52] The importance of understanding just what is meant by the original nature of man and by the instinctive impulses which affect his conduct has been dealt with by James, Thorndike, McDougall, Wallas, Dewey, Shand, Parker and Tead.[53] The significance of suggestion as a factor in social and political processes has been revealed by Sidis,

[50] Comte, *Principles of a Positive Polity,* Vols. III–IV.—For a brief survey of the development of social psychology, cf. *Sociological Review,* Vol XIII, pp. 152-6.

[51] Tarde, *The Laws of Imitation;* and *Social Laws;* Baldwin, *Social and Ethical Interpretations in Mental Development;* Ross *Social Control;* and *Social Psychology.*

[52] Durkheim, *De la division du travail social;* and *Les règles de la méthode sociologique;* Le Bon, *The Crowd; The Psychology of Peoples;* and *The Psychology of Revolutions;* Sumner, *Folkways;* Sighele, *Psychologie des sectes;* and *La foule criminelle;* Trotter, *Instincts of the Herd in Peace and War;* Gumplowicz, *Outlines of Sociology.*

[53] James, *Principles of Psychology,* Vol. II, pp. 383 ff.; Thorndike, *The Original Nature of Man;* McDougall, *Introduction to Social Psychology;* Wallas, *The Great Society;* Dewey, *Human*

Davenport, Wallas, and Ross.[54] The part played by sympathy in society and politics, first noted by Aristotle, Polybius, Spinoza, Hume and Adam Smith, has been investigated by Sutherland, Drummond and Giddings.[55] Benjamin Kidd, following Vico and Hegel, has developed the thesis that religion, as "an ultra-rational sanction" for social conduct, has been the most significant of socializing forces.[56] Sumner has shown, with a great mass of concrete illustrative material, the vast influence of custom and tradition in social and political procedure.[57]

While the analysis of non-intellectual factors in the psychology of society has interested the greatest number of writers, there have been no inconsiderable group who have insisted on the importance of rational or intellectual elements in social and political activities. Spencer, Fouillée, De Greef and Novicow have revived the old notion of the contractual basis of social relationships in a more scientific and tenable form.[58] Bagehot has analyzed the contributions of discussion to social and political progress.[59] Ward and Patten have revised hedonism in a somewhat less crude fashion than it appeared in the Ben-

---

Nature and Conduct; Shand, *The Formation of Character;* Parker, *The Casual Laborer and Other Essays;* Tead, *Instincts in Industry.*

[54] Sidis, *The Psychology of Suggestion;* Davenport, *Primitive Traits in Religious Revivals;* Wallas, *Human Nature in Politics;* Ross, *Social Psychology.*

[55] Sutherland, *Origin and Growth of the Moral Instinct;* Drummond, *The Ascent of Man;* Giddings, *Principles of Sociology.*

[56] *Social Evolution.*

[57] *Folkways.*

[58] Spencer, *Man versus the State;* Fouillée, *La science social contemporaine;* De Greef, *Introduction à la sociologie;* Novicow, *Les luttes entre sociétés humaines.*

[59] *Physics and Politics.*

thamite felicific calculus.[60] The necessity for the supremacy of intellectual factors in controlling social progress, particularly through the domination of the state, has
been maintained by Ward, Stein, Hobhouse and Wallas.[61]
Hall has analyzed the socio-political function of morale.[62]
Some effort to construct a synthesis of psychological
factors in society and politics is to be observed in the
study of the genesis of socio-psychic factors by Hall and
Baldwin [63] and in the comprehensive and balanced works
of Ellwood, Cooley, Edman, Baldwin, Hall, Dewey, Lippmann, Giddings, Bogardus, Small and Ross.[64]

5. *The Cultural Factor in Political and Social Evolution*

Perhaps the most original contribution made by sociologists to the problem of the elements in society and the
state lies in the emphasis which they have laid on the importance of cultural factors, considered in their broadest
significance and implications.   In this they have been aided

[60] Ward, *Outlines of Sociology*, Chap. III; and *Pure Sociology*,
pp. 111 ff.; 256 ff.; Patten, *Theory of Social Forces.*

[61] Ward, *Dynamic Sociology*, Vol. II; *Applied Sociology;* and
Outlines of Sociology, Pt. II; Stein, *Die soziale Frage*, pp. 33 ff.;
and *Einführung in die Soziologie*, pp. 340 ff.; Hobhouse, *Development and Purpose;* and *Social Evolution and Political
Theory;* Wallas, *Our Social Heritage.*

[62] *Morâle: the Supreme Standard of Life and Conduct.*

[63] Hall, *Adolescence;* Baldwin, *Mental Development in the
Child and the Race.*

[64] Ellwood, *Sociology in its Psychological Aspects;* Cooley,
Social Process; Edman, *Human Traits;* Baldwin, *The Individual
and Society;* Hall, *Morâle;* Dewey, *Human Nature and Conduct;*
Lippmann, *Preface to Politics; Drift and Mastery;* and *Public
Opinion;* Giddings, "Pluralistic Behavior," loc. cit.; *Bogardus,
Social Psychology;* Ross, *The Principles of Sociology.*

by the students of primitive culture, such as Boas and his school, Marett and Graebner, and by the sociological and cultural historians such as Lamprecht, Breysig, Müller-Lyer and Teggart. These and other writers have made it clear that biological, geographical, economic and psychological factors in society, considered separately, cannot be regarded as possessing a deterministic character. The same races do not produce identical cultural products in different areas or in distinct periods of history; [65] widely differing cultures arise from identical physical environments and highly similar cultures spring up in diverse environments; [66] there is little or no complete economic determination of institutions and alignments, significant as economic factors may be, particularly in modern western society; [67] psychology cannot adequately explain the great diversity of human attitudes and behavior patterns which are to be found among the varied peoples of the earth, in spite of an identical neurological basis for the mind and the essential unity of mental processes.[68]

One must look for something over and beyond these significant factors, taken separately or together, namely, human culture, which is the product of these factors working in different and varying combinations upon the human organism. When used in this sense by such writers, the word "culture" is interpreted in its broadest and most inclusive sense. It is not used in its conventional connotation as something identical with *belles lettres* or æsthetics, but as embodying all the aspects of creative

[65] Cf. Boas, *The Mind of Primitive Man*, Chap. I.
[66] Lowie, *Culture and Ethnology*, Chap. III.
[67] Lippmann, *Public Opinion*, Pts. IV–V.
[68] Lowie, op. cit., Chaps. I–II.

human endeavor—material culture, institutions and fine arts.[69] It is the thesis of representative writers who support this point of view that the recognition of the cultural factor as the dynamic element in history and political evolution is the key to any adequate interpretation of social and political causation. It enables the student to trace the growth of institutions; to estimate the relative effect of the various influences operating to direct the course of historical development; to secure an adequate grasp upon the indirect processes in historical causation and the interaction of the various types of social forces and institutions; to understand the causes of cultural lag, institutional ossification, and the difficulties involved in social change and improvement; to appreciate the problems of individual and social adaptation to cultural change; and to understand the place of the state in social evolution, institutional growth and social control. The state, from this point of view, appears both as a creation of cultural factors, continually changing and recombining within it, and as one of the most conspicuous of cultural institutions in itself. Above all, this type of analysis reveals the relation of the state to the other social institutions, both with regard to the time perspective of evolution and with regard to present function, and furnishes the only possible basis for a scientific estimate of the plans now being put forward for pluralism and functionalism and for the solution of the problem of the relation of the state to other corporate groups. While the cultural analysis has been notably advanced by a number of enterprising sociologists, anthropologists, and historians, the first *system-*

[69] Ogburn, *Social Change,* pp. 3–51.

atic and comprehensive summary of this extremely significant and promising point of view in social science has been the contribution of W. F. Ogburn and Clark Wissler.[70]

The enumeration of sociological contributions to the discussion of the nature and limitations of sovereignty will be reserved for another section; but it may be pointed out here that it is due almost wholly to the studies of sociologists that the notion of sovereignty has been transformed from an *à priori* metaphysical Hegelian absolute of Burgess or a "determinate superior" of Austin, into a mundane concept with definite social, economic, and psychological sources, uses, and limitations. The economic and social foundations of sovereignty, which were well understood by Adams, Calhoun and Madison, have been comprehensively demonstrated by Commons, Giddings, Loria and Stein, while the socio-psychological basis of political authority and obedience has been conclusively set forth by Tarde, Durkheim, Wallas, McDougall, Sumner, and Ross. Even those sociologists who, like Spencer and Novicow, reject the doctrine of sovereignty, defend their position on sociological grounds.[71]

[70] Ibid., passim. Wissler, *Man and Culture;* Cf. also the references in the *Sociological Review,* Vol. XIII, pp. 214–21. A remarkably clear and intelligent summary of the literature of this topic has been brought together by Herskovits and Willey in their article, "The Cultural Approach to Sociology," in *American Journal of Sociology,* Vol. XIX, pp. 188–99.

[71] Cf. below, pp. 126–39.

CHAPTER VI

THE SOCIOLOGICAL CLASSIFICATION AND ANALYSIS OF THE FORMS OF THE STATE AND GOVERNMENT

1. *Nature of the Sociological Approach to Political Classification*

While sociological writers have generally recognized the importance for administrative and legalistic purposes of the distinction between the state and the government, they have consistently and legitimately maintained that both state and government are inseparable parts of the prevailing political system, so that for purposes of sociological analysis it is quite satisfactory to analyze their characteristics conjointly. Hence, sociological classifications and descriptions of political forms normally relate to the political system as a unified whole. In analyzing this subject of the contributions of sociology to the consideration of the forms of the state and government it will perhaps be best, first to take up sociological analyses and interpretations of the conventional classifications of political institutions, then to deal with the original sociological classifications, and finally to discuss briefly the sociological position as to the desirable form of state and government.

The chief difference between the classifications of government and the state by political scientists and sociolo-

gists is that the latter lay more stress on the social processes going on behind and within the state than upon
the distribution of formal authority or the external aspects of the type of administration. Bentley criticizes
the conventional methods of classification as follows: [1]

Set opposite to all these various forms of so-called psychical interpretation, we have a dead political science. It
is a formal study of the most external characteristics of
governing institutions. It loves to classify governments by
incidental attributes, and when all is said and done it cannot
classify them much better now than by lifting up bodily
Aristotle's monarchies, aristocracies, and democracies which
he found significant for Greek institutions, and using them
for measurements of all sorts and conditions of modern government. And since nobody can be very sure but that the
United States is really a monarchy under the classification
or England really a democracy, the classification is not entitled to great respect. Nor do the classifications that make
the fundamental distinction that between despotism and re-
publics fare much better. They lose all sight of the content of the process in some trick point about the form.

Wherever and whenever we study the process (of government) we never get away from the group and class activities, and when we get these group activities properly
stated we come to see that the differences between governments are not fundamental differences or differences of principle, but that they are strictly differences of technique for
the functioning of the interests, that they are adopted because of group needs, and that they will continue to be
changed in accordance with group needs.

The only classification that Bentley suggests is in strict
conformity with his type of analysis. A despotism exists
where group interests and antagonisms are settled by an

[1] *The Process of Government,* pp. 162, 320.

individual.   A pure democracy is to be found where every interest and group can express itself and is represented in a fair and equitable manner.[2]

2. *Sociological Analyses of the Conventional Classifications of the State*

Giddings bases his classification of political control on the assumption that its form is determined by the prevailing social conditions of the time and the attitude of the governing authorities:[3]

Actual day-by-day rule over a politically organized community by a dominant person or group is political government, and according as this rule is arbitrary or responsible, vigorous or weak, efficient or incompetent, government assumes one or another of the various forms with which history acquaints us, and with which we are familiar in current political discussion. The extremes are absolutism and anarchy. Between these extremes are privileged aristocracy, bordering upon absolutism, and radical democracy bordering upon anarchy. Between privileged aristocracy and radical democracy is a democratic republicanism.

He further maintains that, whatever the form of government, *"the few always dominate. . . .* Invariably the few rule, more or less arbitrarily, more or less drastically, more or less extensively. Democracy, even the most radical democracy, is only that state of politically organized mankind in which the rule of the few is least arbitrary and most responsible, least drastic and most con-

[2] Ibid., pp. 305–6, 311 ff.
[3] *The Responsible State*, pp. 25–6.

siderate." [4] Asserting his belief that a democratic republic is the most perfect of governments,[5] Giddings analyzes in some detail what he means by democracy. He finds that it is more than a form of government. It is not only a form of government, of the state, and of society, but, as a combination of all three of these, it is a stage in the evolution of society and civilization.[6] While vigorously denying Lecky's assertion that democracy is inevitably the rule of the weak, ignorant and vacillating masses, he admits the many weaknesses of contemporary democracy. But, as he well points out, these evils are not the result of the rule of the masses, but the result of the failure of the masses to assert their power and of their "deference to the great humbugs and great scoundrels, and so lend support to Mr. Lecky's belief that democracy is the rule of ignorance, and afford apparent justification of Mr. Carlyle's definition of the people as a certain number of millions, mostly fools." [7]

Again, Giddings is almost the only sociologist who has maintained that democracy can be harmonized with overseas expansion and the development of imperialism. Believing that "democracy and empire" are the two outstanding political developments of the modern age, he has defended expansionism as doubly beneficial, bringing an advanced civilization to backward peoples, and improving

[4] Ibid., pp. 19–20.
[5] Ibid., pp. 33 ff.
[6] *Elements of Sociology,* Chap. XXIV; *Democracy and Empire,* p. 200.—The various phases of democracy which appear to a sociological student are more thoroughly classified and analyzed in the article on "Democracy," by Charles A. Ellwood, in the new edition of the *Encyclopedia Americana.*
[7] *Democracy and Empire,* pp. 199 ff., 213.

government at home through the sobering responsibility that imperial dominion brings with it. He has called upon the American people to assume their part in the "white man's burden" by taking over, administering and civilizing the late Spanish possessions in the Pacific and by erecting thereby a barrier against the advance of the "hordes of Asian barbarism." [8]   Finally, he has carried his doctrine of homogeneity over into the interpretation of democracy and contended that neither in domestic politics nor in imperial administration can liberal political institutions exist without a high development of likemindedness in the population.   But this does not exclude the possibility of a democratic empire, for it is not ethnic likeness that is required, but a sufficient cultural homogeneity, so that the different peoples will be able to agree upon a given set of political institutions and a common type of administrative procedure.[9]

Sumner agreed with Giddings in his criticism of the fallacies of pure democracy as a form of government and in his eulogy of a representative democracy which relies chiefly on the aristocracy of talent for its direction.[10] He differed sharply with Giddings, however, over the possibility of reconciling democracy with imperialism.   He contended that the two are mutually exclusive and that the issue involved in imperialism "is nothing less than whether to go on and maintain our political system or to

[8] Ibid., pp. 1, 269–90, 356–7.

[9] *Elements of Sociology*, pp. 218–21; *Inductive Sociology*, pp. 225 ff.

[10] *Earth Hunger*, p. 88; *The Challenge of Facts*, pp. 226–7, 255–86.

discard it for the European military and monarchical tradition. It must be a complete transformation of the
former to try to carry on under it two groups of political
societies, one on a higher, the other on a lower plane, unequal in rights and powers; the former ruling the latter
perhaps by military force." [11]

Hobhouse also agrees with Giddings and Sumner that
any such thing as pure or direct democratic government
is compatible only with small local units and cannot be applied to large national states.[12] There are also great difficulties to be faced in attempting to operate a democratic
state with a representative republican government. The
issues to be dealt with in modern society are exceedingly
complex. Effective leadership is essential, and democracy
is the least adapted of all forms of political organization
to bring real leaders to the front and the most prone to
fertility in producing demagogues and cheap politicians
who exploit rather than guide the people. Democracy
requires a well-developed common will and a highly organized and intelligent public opinion; but this is difficult
of attainment, and the foremost agency in educating public opinion, the press, is now chiefly engaged in confusing
and deceiving the people. The system of checks and balances in modern democratic governments places the checks
entirely on progressive tendencies and none at all on reactionary policies. Social and economic inequalities persist and help to defeat the substance as well as the form
of democracy. Modern imperialism, as exemplified in the
colonial policies of modern states, is perhaps the most

[11] *War and Other Essays,* pp. 292, 346.
[12] *Democracy and Reaction,* pp. 148–50.

deadly and persistent enemy of democracy at home as well as abroad. Finally, as if the inherent difficulties in democracy were not sufficient, we find the professional politicians deliberately manipulating public opinion and conducting public affairs with the end-in-view of defeating at every turn a truly popular government.[13]

In spite of all these defects and obstacles, however, Hobhouse holds that the burden of proof rests upon any theorist who contends that a more promising and desirable form of political organization than democracy can be found.[14] It need not be assumed that democracy will produce a more efficient government than a specialized bureaucracy, but it carries with it greater assurance of developing the human personality and expressing political right. Further, English experience has completely disproved the assertion that democracy immediately plays into the hands of the rabble, for the Conservative Party was in power more frequently after than before the suffrage extensions of 1867 and 1884. Much could probably be done to remedy the defects in democracy by extending the powers and responsibilities of local government units which are better adapted than large areas to the requirements of democracy.[15] But no true social scientist can hold that democracy is absolutely the best government for

[13] Hobhouse, *Democracy and Reaction*, pp. 49 ff.; 119–23, 148 ff.; *Liberalism*, pp. 183–4, 228 ff.; 242 ff.; *Social Evolution and Political Theory*, pp. 191–2.—I have analyzed Hobhouse's views on democracy more thoroughly in an article on his political theory in the *American Journal of Sociology*, Vol. XXVII. pp. 442–85.

[14] *Democracy and Reaction*, pp. 186–7.

[15] Ibid., pp. 85, 185–7; cf. also *Liberalism*, pp. 228 ff.

all peoples at all times; government is a function of social evolution, and if democracy does not work well in the modern political world it is because the society of the present day is not yet ready for democratic political institutions.[16]

Another eminent sociologist who, with certain qualifications and reservations, is an upholder of democracy is Ludwig Stein. Standing as the exponent of the efficient and constructive democracy of Switzerland, he denies Le Bon's contention that the masses are entirely devoid of reason and that democracy signifies mob rule.[17] He has no patience, however, with the popular dogma of democracy that all men are created equal. It is one of the primary contentions of sociology that men are of unequal ability; and while a state and government may be adjusted to these inequalities, they can never eliminate them. Equality of all in their rights before the law is as far as the dogma of equality can be carried. Democracy is based on the leadership of the aristocracy of talent quite as much as a monarchy.[18]

One of the best sociological analyses of democracy is that contained in the works of Charles H. Cooley. He contends, with a large degree of justification, that the time has arrived when we should cease to discuss the merits of democracy as compared with monarchy or aristocracy. The modern world is becoming a democratic world and democracy must be regarded as an established fact. "Dis-

[16] *Morals in Evolution,* pp. 32 ff.; *Social Evolution and Political Theory,* pp. 127 ff.

[17] Stein, *Die soziale Frage,* pp. 542 ff.

[18] Ibid., pp. 231, 301–2; also "Autoritat," in Schmoller's *Jahrbuch,* 1902, p. 19.

cussion regarding the comparative merits of monarchy, aristocracy and democracy has come to be looked upon as scholastic. The world is clearly democratizing; it is only a question of how fast the movement can take place, and what, under various conditions, it really involves." [19] He denies that democracy in any way means mob-rule; [20] nor is it necessarily a deadly obstacle to the appearance of men and works of genius. De Tocqueville's contention that democracy led to a dead-level of mediocrity was due to his error in assigning this result to the effect of democracy when, in reality, it was an outcome of the confusion incident upon a great transitional age in the development of American society and civilization. [21] Nor can one judge the effects of democracy from the experience of the United States up to the present date; unequal distribution of wealth, the domination of society by the wealthy classes, and the confusion caused by the rapid exploitation of a new country by a growing society, have prevented any extensive actual realization of democracy in this country. [22]

Viewed in its most fundamentally sociological and psychological sense, democracy is not "a single and definite political type," but is an ambitious and desirable attempt to extend to great modern national states the application of the primary ideals of loyalty, truth, service, kindness, lawfulness, freedom, and justice, which were developed in the primary groups of the family, neighbor-

[19] *Social Organization,* p. 120.
[20] Ibid., pp. 149 ff.
[21] Ibid., pp. 159 ff.
[22] Ibid., pp. 162 ff.; 256 ff.

hood and local community.[23]   Upon the success of this
effort depends the future of democracy.   Cooley agrees
that direct political democracy is not possible in large
states, and that representative government is inevitable.
This, he says, necessitates able leaders, and he analyzes
with real acumen the factors involved in leadership and
its recognition and utilization by the public.[24]   While the
leaders must furnish social guidance in a democracy, the
masses function through their expression of public sentiment—something for which the common people are better
fitted than the business and professional classes.[25]   The
masses make this contribution through the choice of
leaders, whose wisdom is manifested by their ability to
interpret and apply this popular sentiment.   "The sentiment of the people is most readily and successfully exercised in their judgment of persons. . . . The plainest
men have an inbred shrewdness in judging human nature which makes them good critics of persons even when
impenetrable to ideas. . . . On this shrewd judgment of
persons the advocate of democracy chiefly grounds his
faith that the people will be right in the long run." [26]
Thus democracy is a social system and a political order
in which the masses "contribute sentiment and common
sense, which give momentum and general direction to
progress, and as regards particulars find their way by a

[23] Ibid., pp. 23–57, 85–6, 118–20.—The difficulties involved in
this process are far more adequately realized and more effectively
set forth by Lippmann, in his *Public Opinion.*
[24] *Social Organization,* pp. 146, 404; *Human Nature and the
Social Order,* pp. 283–325.
[25] *Social Organization,* pp. 135–48.
[26] Ibid., pp. 142–3.

shrewd choice of leaders." [27]   With an enviable opti-
mism Cooley concludes that the facts of history and social
science sanction a belief in the efficacy and permanence
of democracy.[28]

Set off against these sociologists, who are qualified de-
fenders of democracy, are those who, for widely different
reasons, criticize democratic institutions, or at least the
modern approximations to democratic institutions. Le
Bon has presented a series of indictments of democracy,
particularly French democracy, alleging that it tends to
degenerate into mob-rule, that it does not give sufficient
play to the element of talent, and that it follows political
phantoms, especially the phantom of state socialism.[29]
Faguet has bitterly arraigned democracy because of its
incapacity to enlist the services of the true aristocracy of
talent, and its fatal willingness to rely on the leadership
of the mediocre, or the scoundrels and rascals that dominate contemporary partisan politics.[30]   Mallock has been
equally caustic in his denunciation of liberal democracy, on
the grounds that it is opposed by the doctrines of biological evolution, that it ignores talent and runs counter to
the authoritarianism and orientation of the Roman
Catholic Church.[31] Gumplowicz, Oppenheimer, Small,
and Loria, though sympathetic with democracy, have

[27] Ibid., p. 148.

[28] Cooley's analysis of democracy should be compared with
the more realistic investigation of the problem by Walter Lippmann in his *Public Opinion.*

[29] *The Crowd; Psychology of Socialism;* and *La psychologie
politique.*

[30] *The Cult of Incompetence.* Cf. also Ludovici, *A Defence
of Aristocracy.*

[31] *Social Equality; The Limits of Pure Democracy; Aristocracy and Evolution;* and *A Critical Examination of Socialism.*

shown the relation which exists between property and politics, and have contended that no true political democracy can exist so long as gross inequalities of property and economic power persist, and so long as individuals are allowed to go on with the exploitation of land and labor.[32] Loria, in commenting on the popularity of the first edition of his *Economic Foundations of Society,* says on this point: [33]

I must refer the success of the book to the perfect frankness with which it denounced the enormities of contemporary morals and politics, and set the plain truth over against the systematic falsification of things so common to modern sociologists. The book revealed the secret to the world: it boldly declared what no one had had the courage to say, that cupidity, narrow mean egoism and class spirit ruled in our so-called democracies; it ruthlessly unmasked the political deities that the world had been in the habit of invoking with pompous phrases, and, raising the veil that covered them, it showed that where we had expected to find mystical Isis, there was only a yawning greedy crocodile.

As will be shown below in greater detail, some penetrating sociological students of democracy have held that democracy is threatened by the party system, with its organization, oligarchical tendencies, perversions of means into ends, and its facilitation of appeals to irrational emotions rather than to the critical judgment of the population. This line of criticism, which has been urged in particular

[32] Gumplowicz, *Outlines of Sociology,* pp. 121, 123, 132, 144–6; Oppenheimer, *The State,* Chaps. I, VI–VII; Small, *Between Eras: From Capitalism to Democracy;* Loria, *The Economic Foundations of Society,* translated by L. M. Keasby, pp. 73 ff.; 119 ff.

[33] Op. cit., Preface, p. xi.

by Wallas and Michels,[34] and has been executed more
in detail by publicists such as Bryce and Ostrogorski, has
suggested that our modern democracy under the party
system bears a considerable resemblance to medieval
feudalism with the absence of the land element. From
the biological standpoint aristocracy has been defended
against democracy by Galton, de Lapouge, Ammon, and
Schallmayer.[35]   From a bio-psychic standpoint Mc-
Dougall, Goddard, Lichtenberger, Hankins, Stoddard and
others have questioned the democratic dogma of the
equality of man and have indicated the danger of a trend
toward mediocrity or inferiority in majority rule.   Of
late they have secured significant data from the mental
tests given to the American soldiers during the recent
World War.[36]

Probably the most trenchant and constructive critique
of the modern democratic dogma and practice, chiefly

[34] Wallas, *Human Nature in Politics;* Michels, *Political Parties.*

[35] Cf. their works cited above, p. 61.

[36] McDougall, *Is America Safe for Democracy?"* Lichtenberger, "The Social Significance of Mental Levels," in *Publications of the American Sociological Society,* Vol. XV, 1920;
Goddard, *Human Efficiency and Levels of Intelligence;* Yerkes
and Yoakum, *The Army Mental Tests.*—A comprehensive work
on this subject is in preparation by F. H. Hankins. While
Lichtenberger and Goddard formally defend democracy, the
evidence of their data naturally leads to the opposite conclusion;
and history offers little confirmation of the allegation that majority rule produces the best leadership.   For a critique of the deduc-
tions from the army intelligence tests, cf. the series of articles
by Walter Lippmann in *The New Republic,* beginning Oct. 25,
1922, which should be compared with an authoritative and mod-
erate article by E. G. Boring in *The New Republic,* June 6, 1923,
pp. 35–37.

from a socio-psychological point of view, has been contributed by Walter Lippmann. So distinguished an authority as John Dewey hazards the opinion that "it is perhaps the most effective indictment of democracy as currently conceived ever penned." Lippmann's argument may be briefly summarized as follows: The effectiveness and reality of democracy depend upon the adequacy of public opinion as a guide to political policy and action. The early democratic dogma, and the beginnings of democratic practice, were based upon the notions, ideals, problems, and practices of the small, rural, self-governing local community. To such conditions the spontaneously generated public opinion was reasonably well adapted, and the average individual was here relatively "omni-competent" in political action. Some democratic theorists, as, for example, Jefferson, understood this and agreed that the permanence and success of democracy depended upon the ability to preserve the vitality and ascendency of the simple agrarian community. But this has not been possible. Modern industrialism has produced the complexity of urban life, racial and cultural intermixture, world contacts in politics and commerce, and an unprecedented volume of new and difficult problems, both national and international. Yet we have naïvely attempted to operate this complicated modern political and social machinery on the basis of the skill and rules drawn from the period of primitive agrarian simplicity. In the place of expert guidance, founded upon prolonged and objective research, we have been willing to remain almost ostentatiously, if fatally, content to be dominated by custom, tradition, stupid censorship, or cunningly devised propaganda—all alike characterized by an all-pervading ignorance and a derivation from a pre-industrial and pre-scientific age. Until we are able to organize and support an adequate body of public experts to secure for legislators, administrators, and citizens the greatest possible array of well verified facts for the political guidance and educational equipment of citizens, we can hope for no efficiency or practical success in modern democratic society.[37]

The criticisms of democracy by such writers as Treitschke and Sybel, which were based upon a near "divine-right" eulogy of a particular dynasty, and a racial theory of politics, may be regarded as too obviously anachronistic to deserve analysis or refutation.[38]

In concluding the discussion of sociological analyses of the conventional types of state and government, it may be emphasized that all these writers argue that any valid classification must be founded upon and related to general social conditions and circumstances. While the majority agree that democracy is the most promising type of political organization, they all admit that there are certain definite sociological prerequisites for the success of any democratic experiment; those who look with disfavor upon democracy also base their indictment upon sociological grounds. In short, all contend that forms and types of states and governments depend directly upon general and fundamental social conditions and circumstances.

[37] Lippmann, *Public Opinion,* passim, esp. Pts. I, V–VI. Cf. also the magisterial and indispensable review of the book by John Dewey, *The New Republic,* May 3, 1922, pp. 286–8.

[38] Treitschke, *Politics;* Sybel, *History of the French Revolution.*

3. *Sociological Classifications of the State*

It is because of this conviction that an intimate relation exists between the type of society and the form of the state and government that many sociologists have tended to supplement the conventional classifications or to add new ones of their own with sociological implications. Comte maintained that there were but two fundamental types of political control—a theocracy, where the temporal power was subordinate to the spiritual, and a sociocracy, where the temporal and spiritual power were properly coordinated.[39] Spencer, with genesis as well as analysis in his mind, divided states into two great successive types, the military and the industrial.[40] In the first and earliest type the organization was fashioned primarily for efficiency in war, political control was highly authoritative, and state activity was extensive within certain ranges. In the second and latest type productive industry is the basis of social organization, political control is democratic, individual liberty extensive, and state activity is severely limited. Bagehot suggested a classification related to Spencer's when he divided the historic states into two types, those based on authoritative control and specialized for war, and those founded on the principle of government by discussion.[41]

Akin to these also is the classification adopted by Ratzenhofer and Small, namely, the earlier "conquest-state," based on the subjection of one group by another through

[39] *Principles of a Positive Polity,* Vol. II, p. 344.
[40] *The Principles of Sociology,* Vol. II, pp. 568 ff.
[41] *Physics and Politics.*

physical force, and the "culture-state," where political
control is more liberal and tempered by industrial development.[42]   Within this latter type of state Small dis-
tinguishes the present capitalistic state, characterized by
a combination of "lottery and famine" and real democracy,
which must include social and economic, as well as political, democracy.   Just now we are in an intermediate stage
between capitalism and democracy.[43]   Somewhat related,
too, is Durkheim's genetic division of society and the state
into territorial, repressive and mechanical in the earlier
stages, and functional, liberal and organic in its developed
phase.[44]   Ward suggested that while monarchy, aristocracy and democracy might constitute a satisfactory conventional classification of states, it is necessary to distinguish three phases or stages of modern democracy.[45]   The
first is physiocracy, or that extreme individualism which
rested upon an alleged political analogy with Newtonian
mechanics; the second, plutocracy, or the control of politics by organized and predatory wealth; and the third,
sociocracy, or the control of society by legislators who are
social scientists and who consciously devise ways for
achieving and accelerating social progress according to
the laws of sociology.

Hobhouse would differentiate political types according
to the basic principle of political cohesion.[46]   There are
three such successive principles: kinship; authority,

[42] Small, *General Sociology,* pp. 193 ff.
[43] *Between Eras: From Capitalism to Democracy.*
[44] *De la division du travail social.*
[45] *The Psychic Factors of Civilization,* pp. 311–23.
[46] *Morals in Evolution,* pp. 42 ff.

which may be exercised in absolute monarchies, feudal monarchies and empires; and citizenship, which is the foundation of the modern democratic national state. Tarde, with his penchant for psychological criteria, holds that there are but two vital forms of political control—a "téléocratie" and an "idéocratie." [47] The former is based on a domination of desires and is illustrated by the governments of dictators and military adventurers. The latter is founded upon the sovereignty of ideas and beliefs and is manifested by doctrinaire governments. At present the tendency seems to be toward the triumph of the ideocracy, which is the highest of these two forms of government. Ross also doubts the significance of the conventional classifications of governmental power "for the location of social power expresses much more truly the inner constitution of society than does the location of political power.[48] And so the shiftings of power within the state, far from having causes of their own, are apt to follow and answer to the shifting of power within society. Yet, since political power is palpable and lies near the surface of things, political science long ago ascertained its forms and laws; while social power, lying hidden in the dim depths, has hardly even yet drawn the attention of social science." Ross presents a preliminary classification of the different types of social régimes based upon the concentration of social power: [49]

[47] *Les transformations du pouvoir*, pp. 212-3. Cf. also *Philosophical Review*, May, 1919.

[48] *Social Control*, pp. 78-9.

[49] Ibid. Professor Giddings' elaborate classification of the different types of societies, which possesses significance for politics, is reproduced in full below, pp. 210-14.

In some cases there exists an appropriate name for the régime. When the priest guides it we call it *clericalism*. When the fighting caste is deferred to, we call it *militarism*. When the initiative lies with the minions of the state we call it *officialism*. The leadership of moneyed men is *capitalism*. That of men of ideas is *liberalism*. The reliance of men upon their own wisdom and strength is *individualism*.

These distinctions, I need hardly add, are far deeper than distinctions like aristocracy, monarchy, republic, which relate merely to the form of government.

An economic orientation is seen in the classification proposed by Commons.[50] He denies that a despotism can properly be regarded as a state. It is but a private patrimony. Aristocracy is based upon government through hereditary property, while plutocracy is government by transferable property. Democracy is government by universal suffrage. Loria presents a somewhat unusual economic interpretation of the forms of political control.[51] If the prevailing revenue or source of material gain is concentrated in the hands of a few men, aristocracy will exist; if it is distributed among a large number, a monarchy, more or less absolute at the pleasure of the dominant class, will prevail. When, however, the revenue is bifurcated and divided between two powerful classes a struggle for power will follow, and the government must be liberal and flexible enough to allow this struggle to proceed. In other words, a democracy will result; and modern democracies are primarily a result of the struggles between landowners and capitalists. Oppenheimer

[50] "A Sociological View of Sovereignty," in *American Journal of Sociology*, Vol. V, pp. 362–5.
[51] *The Economic Foundations of Society*, pp. 135–6, 141, 169, 327.

holds that there are two fundamental types of social order, that in which the state is predominant and that in which it is replaced by the "Freeman's Citizenship." In whatever form the state has existed through history it has been but a type of technique for organized and sanctioned robbery—the exploitation of the economic by the political means. It will ultimately be replaced by the Freeman's Citizenship, in which the state will disappear and with it the system of organized plunder which it has sanctioned, if not created.[52]

[52] *The State,* pp. 274 ff.

CHAPTER VII

SOCIOLOGICAL ANALYSES OF THE PROCESSES AND MECHANISM OF GOVERNMENT [1]

1. *Nature of the State and the Government*

In treating the important problem of the real essence of government the sociologists have in most cases abandoned the tendency to remain satisfied with the pious abstraction that government "exists for the good of the governed" or for the advancement of Christian virtues in the community, and have sought to discover the real nature of the "process of government." In doing so they have gone back to the position first established by Aristotle, elaborated by Althusius, and revived in more recent times by John Adams, Madison, Calhoun, Gierke, Maitland, Figgis, Duguit, Laski, and others, namely that society is a complex of groups which are given coherence and energy by the possession of a common interest or set of interests.[2] The state exists to furnish the necessary restraint for this conflict of interests and to insure that it will be a beneficial rather than a destructive proc-

[1] Much more basic and important, of course, than the specific sociological analysis of the governmental process is the sociological synthesis of the factors creating society, state, government, and political doctrine and practice The most profound contribution to this subject is Giddings' above-mentioned paper on "A Theory of Social Causation."

[2] Cf. Beard, *The Economic Basis of Politics.*

ess. Government is the agency through which these groups carry on the public phases of their conflict and secure to a greater or lesser degree the objects of the group interest. In the history of this doctrine there have been two chief lines of development, complementary rather than opposed and unrelated. Gierke, Maitland, Laşki, Duguit, and Durkheim have dealt chiefly with the nature of these groups, their internal organization and status, and their relation to each other and to the state. This study of the form of social groups has culminated in the writings of George Simmel, who has constructed a vast "social geometry." [3] The intra-group and inter-group processes, namely, the origin and nature of group interests, the conflict of these interests and their adjustment, have been studied by Calhoun, Gumplowicz, Ratzenhofer, Oppenheimer, Small, Bentley, and Miss Follett. These two trends, taken together, constitute, perhaps, the most significant contribution made to either political or social theory in the last generation.

2. *The Group Concept of the State*

The first important modern sociological application of this doctrine was made by Gumplowicz.[4] In accordance with the principle of *syngenism,* he contends that groups tend to organize about certain definite interests and to

[3] *Soziologie: Untersuchungen über die Formen der Vergesellschaftung.* This work has appeared in substance in English as articles in the *American Journal of Sociology.* An exposition of Simmel's social and political theory is in preparation by Dr. N. J. Spykman of the University of California.

[4] *Der Rassenkampf* (French translation *La lutte des races*), pp. 241–2; *Outlines of Sociology,* pp. 123 ff.

seek to dominate other groups in order more effectively to realize their common interests. Government is the agency through which the dominant group effects and legalizes the exploitation of the subjected or subordinate groups. This view of the state as the public or legal organ making possible the economic exploitation of society through political means is also shared, among others, by Oppenheimer and Loria.[5] It must be pointed out, however, that none of the writers are orthodox Marxian socialists, and that Gumplowicz himself is a vigorous critic of the whole socialistic philosophy of social reconstruction.

A somewhat less extreme position is taken by Ratzenhofer and Small, who claim that government is the agency through which the state adjusts this conflict of interests and keeps it within legal and pacific bounds, though in undemocratic societies this adjustment may lead to domination and subordination.[6] This view is also adhered to by Bentley.[7] An even more benevolent function is assigned to the government by Vaccaro, who believes that government is chiefly designed to achieve an adaptation and reconciliation of conflicting interests.[8] Finally, in the later writings of Novicow one meets in a slightly different form the doctrine of the old Manchester School that the government fulfils the function of a policeman stationed in a department store by establishing legal

[5] Oppenheimer, *The State*, pp. 24 ff.; 257 ff., Loria, *The Economic Foundations of Society*, pp. 9, 19 ff., 328, 343 ff.

[6] Ratzenhofer, *Wesen und Zweck der Politik;* Small, *General Sociology*, pp. 224 ff.

[7] *The Process of Government*, Chaps. VII, X.

[8] *Les bases sociologiques du droit et de l'état*, pp. 4, 430 ff. See also Bristol, *Social Adaptation*, Introduction, and pp. 313 ff.

methods and protection in the exchange of commodities.[9]

Of these points of view that of Ratzenhofer, Small and Bentley is probably the soundest and most acceptable,[10] and a brief survey of this position may be included on the basis of Bentley's analysis, as this is one of the cardinal contributions of sociology to political theory. Bentley believes that groups of men, held together by definite interests, are the real raw material of politics: [11]

There is no group without its interest. An interest, as the term will be used in this work, is the equivalent of a group. We may speak also of an interest group or of a group interest, again merely for the sake of clearness in expression. The group and the interest are not separate. There exists only the one thing, that is, so many men bound together in or along the path of a certain activity. Sometimes we may be emphasizing the interest phase, sometimes the group phase, but if ever we push them too far apart we soon land in the barren wilderness. There may be a beyond-scientific question as to whether the interest is responsible for the existence of the group, or the group responsible for the existence of the interest. I do not know or care. What we actually find in this world, what we can observe and study, is interested men, nothing more and nothing less. That is our raw material and it is our business to keep our eyes fastened to it. . . .

As for political questions under any society in which we are called upon to study them, we shall never find a group interest of the society as a whole. We shall always find that the political interests and activities of any given group —and there are no political phenomena except group phenomena—are directed against other activities of men who

[9] "The Mechanism and Limits of Human Association," loc. cit.
[10] Cf. an excellent brief summary of this type of analysis in Bristol, *Social Adaptation*, pp. 162 ff.
[11] Bentley, op. cit., pp. 211–12, 222.

appear in other groups, political or other. The phenomena of political life which we study will always divide the society in which they occur, along lines which are very real, though of varying degrees of definiteness. The society itself is nothing other than the complex of the groups that compose it.

As the functions of government are devoted to adjusting these conflicting interests, which exert their pressure through the groups that express these interests, he says further: [12]

There is not a single function of government which is not supported on a powerful interest group or set of groups from which it gets all its strength and social effectiveness. In every such case where two opposing groups have their conflicts adjusted or controlled through a ruler we shall find that the ruler is in reality acting as the leader of an interest group or set of groups more powerful than those in immediate conflict, and that the adjustment and limitation which we observe is dictated by that more powerful group. . . .

In the broadest sense—a very broad sense indeed—government is the process of the adjustment of a set of interest groups in a particular distinguishable group or system. . . .

All phenomena of government are phenomena of groups pressing one another, forming one another, and pushing out new groups and group representatives (the organs or agencies of government) to mediate the adjustments. It is only as we isolate these group activities, determine their representative values, and get the whole process stated in terms of them, that we approach to a satisfactory knowledge of government.

These interest-groups, in order to attain their objects, bring pressure upon the various agencies and organs of

[12] Ibid., pp. 235, 260, 269.

government, and governmental policies, acts, and achievements are but the resultant of the various types of group pressure exerted in this manner.[13]   The relative importance of any department of government depends upon the success with which it is able to adjust these conflicting interests and to mediate between the groups that represent them.[14]   Even the judiciary is not immune to the pressure of these social interests.[15]   Normally, however, the legislature is the great arena in which these interest-groups contend, and the chief method of adjustment is log-rolling, which is the characteristic technique of legislation. [16]

Log-rolling is a term of approbrium.   This is because it is used mainly with reference to its grosser forms. . . . Log-rolling is, however, in fact, the most characteristic legislative process. . . . And when we have reduced the legislative process to the play of group interests, then log-rolling, or give and take, appears as the very nature of the process. It is compromise, not in the abstract moral form, which philosophers can sagely discuss, but in the practical form with which every legislator who gets results through government is acquainted.   It is trading.   It is the adjustment of interests. . . . There was never a time in the history of the American congress when legislation was conducted in any other way.

3. *Reconstruction of Representative Government*

As has been made clear above, sociologists for the most part believe that direct government, either monarchical or

[13] Ibid., pp. 330 ff.
[14] Ibid., p. 359.
[15] Ibid., pp. 388 ff.   Cf. also, Myers, *History of the Supreme Court.*
[16] Bentley, op. cit., pp. 370–1.

democratic, is either undesirable or impossible, and that representative government is the only feasible type. In dealing with the problem of representative government the question arises as to what shall constitute the basis of representation and what shall be the representative units. Are economic and professional interests to be the basis of representation, as was the case in medieval and early modern times, or the territorial unit of population, as has developed in more recent times, partly as a result of the political dogmas of Rousseau and partly as a consequence of the growth of certain conceptions and practices associated with the development of modern democracy, especially in America? Among the sociologists who have given special attention to this subject there are but few, as might be expected, who defend the present illogical and artificial method of representation by territorial units, based, as it is, upon the political and psychological fallacy that there is a general community or district sentiment, apart from the interests of the various classes and groups, which can be isolated and represented in government.[17] They have demonstrated the fact that even under territorial representation the basic interests group seek, and in various indirect or subterranean ways obtain, that representation which is denied to them in a direct and open form. Lobbying and log-rolling become the essential method of representative government even under the most perfect system of territorial representation. Indeed, most sociologists, in common with progressive po-

[17] The only notable recent defense of territorialism is to be found in Wallas, *Our Social Heritage,* Chaps. V–VI. Cf. also Sidney and Beatrice Webb, *A Constitution for a Socialist Commonwealth of Great Britain.*

litical scientists, agree that the adjustment of group interests is the essential process of government; hence, representative government should bring its forms and mechan-
isms into harmony with the real purpose and function of
politics. Further, the social psychologists have finally laid
at rest the Rousseauean dogma relative to the general
will of a community, which scarcely may be said to exist
except in times of a social crisis involving a great common danger; and his other dogmatic support of territorial representation, namely, what might be called his
capitation theory of distributive sovereignty, has even
fewer supporters.[18]

The sociologists who favor the revival in a more scientific and democratic form of the direct representation of
interests answer the chief objection to this proposal,
namely, that it will bring class and group selfishness, confusion and obstruction, by holding that the same classes
and groups now seek and achieve this representation by
indirect and circuitous methods. Group selfishness exists to as great a degree now as it could with any other
system of representation, while the creation of direct opportunity for group representation would clarify and ex-
pedite matters. In fact, it might even be hoped that it
would in some measure diminish group selfishness, which
among many groups and classes has been intensified by
long-continued frustration of their aims and interests.
To the final objection that it would be impossible to apply
this system of representation in practice, even if it were

[18] The clearest presentation, known to the writer, of the case
for the representation of interests is contained in an article by
H. A. Overstreet, "The Government of Tomorrow," in *The
Forum*, Vol. LIV, pp. 6–17.

ethically and logically desirable, its adherents answer that this is the most threadbare and fallacious argument in the whole history of politics, having haunted every innovation from the first establishment of the tribal chieftainship to the passage of the English Reform Bill of 1832 and the granting of universal suffrage.

Among the sociologists who have argued directly for the representation of interests rather than of territorial units have been Schäffle, Le Prins, Benoist, De Greef, Durkheim, and the Gild Socialists.[19] The doctrine is logically inseparable from the related theories of Gumplowicz, Oppenheimer, Loria, Ratzenhofer, Small, and Bentley, and, to a lesser extent, from those of Gierke, Maitland, Laski and Duguit. Durkheim has pointed out that the territorial unit may be retained with some logical function and *rationale* as the district from which the representatives of the professional or occupational classes or groups may be chosen. Duguit, on the other hand, would combine territorial and functional representation by having a bi-cameral legislature in which one house would be chosen by territorial and the other by functional groups.[20] Perhaps the clearest statement of the case for vocational representation has been made by H. A. Overstreet in an article entitled "The Government of Tomorrow:"[21]

[19] Schäffle, *Bau und Leben des socialen Körpers;* Le Prins, *Le démocratie et le régime représentatif;* Benoist, *La crise de l'état moderne;* De Greef, *La constituante et le régime représentatif;* Durkheim, *De la division du travail social,* second edition, 1902, Preface; *Le suicide,* pp. 343 ff.; Cole, *Social Theory,* Chap. VIII.—For more recent discussions, cf. Beard, *The Economic Basis of Politics,* pp. 46 ff.; and McBain and Rogers, *New Constitutions of Europe,* Chap. VI.

[20] Durkheim, op. cit.; Duguit, *Traité de droit constitutionnel.*

[21] Cf. the *Forum,* Vol. LIV, pp. 7, 11, 16, 17.

One of the most serious defects of our political machinery is found in the prevalent theory of representation. It is curious how contentedly we accept that theory as if it had been handed to us from Sinai's top, not noting that the times have so changed as to make the theory no longer truly applicable. We view it as a matter of course that a political state should be divided into its smaller units, and these into still smaller; and that in each unit citizens should vote as members of the unit. Thus the group of people who constitute precinct eleven of district four of the borough of Manhattan recognize, as a matter of course, that their political identity lies in their membership within those territorial boundaries. The person who "represents" these citizens represents them as inhabitants of that particular territory. . . .

The significant change that has occurred is that territorial propinquity is no longer coincident with community of interest. This change is wholly crucial. It means that where political life could be successfully organized in terms of land occupation, such organization is now in large measure artificial and ineffective. Community of interest is now determined fundamentally by specific vocation. A physician living in the eleventh precinct has far more community of interest with a physician living in the fifth precinct than he has with the broker who lives around the corner. Indeed, if one were to trace the lines of interest demarcation in a great city, one would find them here, there, and everywhere, crossing and recrossing all the conventional political boundaries. If one seeks, in short, the natural groupings in our modern world, one finds them in the associations of teachers, of merchants, of manufacturers, of physicians, of artisans. The Trade Union, the Chamber of Commerce, the Medical Association, the Bar Association, the Housewives' League—these even in their half-formed state are the forerunners of the true political units of the modern state.

Always, in history, political effectiveness has had its source in common understanding, in common enthusiasm.

Where men work at the same trade, or pursue the same business, or follow the same profession, there is an identity of interest that makes for group solidarity and power. A perfectly clear principle of psychology is here involved. Where two or three are gathered together who are of widely diverse interests, there can be little save trivial talk of the times and of the weather. When, on the contrary, there are gathered together those who are of like interest and understanding, there results a mutual enhancement which makes for the greater power of each and of all. The weakness and timid superficiality of our political life of today are due, in large measure, to the fact that the state is made up of groups of the first—the talk-of-the-weather type. Our political life will come to idealistic power only when the state is transformed into groups of the second—the organic type.

The objection is often raised that occupational grouping would simply mean a battle of interests—each group fighting for itself. In the first place, matters, in this respect, could scarcely be worse than they are now. In the second place, groups such as we have indicated are not, in their interests, antagonistic. Housewives are not antagonistic to physicians; nor carpenters to teachers; nor ministers of religion to outdoor unskilled workers. As a matter of fact, the interests of many of these groups coalesce, as in the case of housewives, teachers, physicians, etc. But what is significant is that, with as many occupational groups as we have indicated, no constant balancing of interest one over against the other would be possible—as would be the case, for example, if the occupational groups were, as has elsewhere been suggested, farmers, merchants, clerics. . . .

It would be folly, of course, to pretend that a high grade of political efficiency will be attained at once when men change from the anorganic system of territorial to the organic system of vocational grouping. But it may at least be maintained, with some show of reason, that with that change one of the most insidiously persistent obstacles to political efficiency will have been removed.

4. *Separation of Governmental Powers*

Equally divergent from the conventional views is the sociological position as to the separation of governmental powers which has long held a mythological position as the chief guardian of political liberty and legal justice. Following progressive writers on historical and analytical politics,[22] sociologists have agreed that this doctrine arose out of a grotesque misinterpretation of the English government by Montesquieu, and that it has proved no less unworkable in practice than it was erroneous and fallacious in origin. From the sociological point of view government appears as a unified process and not as a static product of Newtonian mechanics or a physical equilibrium. As Bentley and others have conclusively shown, all branches and agencies of government are devoted to one or another phase of the adjustment of group interests, and no branch can logically be regarded as existing to oppose the other. Further, the importance of different departments of government continually fluctuates in accordance with the intensity and incidence of group pressure and the success of the department in adjusting the conflicting group interests.[23] Cole and the Gild Socialists contend that there can be no logical division of governmental powers by departments or stages, but only according to the function to be performed.[24] Tarde, from the psychological point of view, ridicules the notion of the separation of powers as a guaranty of political liberty and

[22] Cf. Goodnow, *Politics and Administration;* Ford, *Rise and Growth of American Politics;* Powell, "The Separation of Power," loc. cit.

[23] Cf. Bentley, op. cit., pp. 235, 258 ff., 330 ff., 359.

[24] Cf. Cole, *Social Theory,* pp. 124-5.

contends that the only bulwark against oppression lies in the independence of beliefs and desires in the individual mind. The customs of the group, which furnish the individual with his beliefs, prevent him from following out the line of conduct dictated by his desires. If this were not true, all government would develop into unlimited tyranny.[25]   Ward calls for a far greater degree of executive leadership in the legislature, and would have executive policy determined by the advice of a body of sociologists who would investigate the problems of society through statistical measurement and recommend measures and policies according to sociological principles.[26]

5. *Decentralization of the State*

Various writers, notably Durkheim, would separate administration in part from the central political government. They would allow the central government to decide general policies, but would put the specific application of these policies in the hands of the various professional and occupational groups which possess the specialized knowledge essential to intelligent administration. This attitude has been much more thoroughly proposed and discussed by the administrative syndicalists.[27]   The Gild Socialists would go even further and hand over legislative functions concerning all groups of producers to such organizations, reserving political legislation and administration

[25] *Les transformations du pouvoir,* pp. 160 ff.
[26] *The Psychic Factors of Civilization,* pp. 309–27; *Dynamic Sociology,* Vol. II, pp. 245 ff.; *Outlines of Sociology,* pp. 278–9; *Glimpses of the Cosmos,* Vol. II, pp. 167–71.
[27] Cf. Durkheim, loc. cit.; also Laski, *Authority in the Modern State;* and Buell, *Contemporary French Politics,* Chap. XI.

chiefly for the activities and relations of the citizens as consumers.[28] The Syndicalists would abolish the state and provide a system of social control based on government through strengthened and federated trade-unions.[29]

There are also some sociologists who believe that the most desirable remedial reform in governmental procedure would be to increase the powers and responsibilities of local units. They feel that the great national states are artificial and overgrown political entities, and that the incompetence of modern governments and the indifference of the people to political problems are largely due to the attempt to confer upon large political units such powers as can be effectively exercised only by small communities or integral groups that are in close touch with the problems involved and are responsive to the questions at issue. These writers advocate the establishment of the organic community or the natural group as the basis of political and social life, and would secure the advantages of protection and uniformity of general policy, which are best to be found in a large political group, by providing for a federation of the communities in a general political unity.[30] Miss Follett has well summarized the point of view which she advocates: [31]

28 Cf. Cole, op. cit., pp. 117–57.
29 Cf. Mott, "The Political Theory of Syndicalism," loc. cit.
30 Cf. MacIver, *Community: a Sociological Study;* Geddes, *Cities in Evolution;* Geddes and Branford, *The Coming Polity;* Follett, *The New State;* Brun, *Le régionalisme.* MacIver and, to a lesser extent, Miss Follett use the term community to describe a group united by common interests, traditions, and understanding, while Geddes and the regionalists stress the geographic region, which they believe produces a natural unity of life and interests.
31 Op. cit., pp. 6, 10, 301–3.

We find the true man only through group organization. The potentialities of the individual remain potentialities until they are released by group life. Man discovers his true nature, gains his true freedom, only through the group. Group organization must be the new method of politics, because the modes by which the individual can be brought forth and made effective are the modes of practical politics. . . .

Some of the pluralists tend to lose the individual in the group; others to abandon the state for the group. But the individual, the group, the state—they are all there to be reckoned with—we can not ignore or minimize any one. The relation of individual to group, of group to group, of individual and group to state—the part that labor is to have in the new state—these are the questions to the consideration of which this book is directed. . . .

Federalism must live through: (1) the reality of the group, (2) the expanding group, (3) the ascending group or unifying process. The federal state is the unifying state. . . . Federalism is the only possible form for the state because it leaves room for the new forces which are coming, for the myriad centers of life which must be forever springing up, group after group, within a vital state. Our impulse is at one and the same time to develop self and to transcend self. It is this ever transcending self which needs the federal state. . . . Thus it is the federal state which expresses the two fundamental principles of life—the compounding of consciousness and the endless appearings of new forces.

6. *Sociological Analyses of the Political Party*

The sociologists look upon the political party, not as a spontaneous and voluntary benevolent association—the political manifestation of the *logos*—but as the public organization through which interest-groups seek to promote their specific objects and ambitions.[32] The party is an interest-group or a combination of interest-groups in an organization which can advance in a more powerful way the aspirations of the component groups. If the party represents a combination of interest-groups, and at the same time is a coherent and well disciplined party, the specific interests of the constituent groups must have more common than divergent elements and objectives, or the party will sooner or later disintegrate. Interest-groups must compromise with one another in organizing in a great party, precisely as compromise is essential in legislation and the final adjustment of interests in governmental action. On this account considerable latitude must be given in party platforms, or whatever serves as the basis of party unity. The strongest parties are those which can unite the greatest number of individuals in a single interest-group or can most successfully combine in a harmonious manner, without sacrificing aggressiveness, the largest number of interest-groups. This conception of the political party has been concisely summarized by Bentley: [33]

[32] Michels has well stated the compensatory tendency of political parties to represent their program as conceived in the interest of society at large and to deny any special party or class aims: "Political parties, however much they may be founded upon narrow class interests and however evidently they may work against the interests of the majority, love to identify themselves with the universe, or at least to present themselves as cooperating with all the citizens of the state and to proclaim that they are fighting in the name of all and for the good of all." (*Political Parties,* p. 16.)

[33] Op. cit., p. 225. Cf. also Small, *General Sociology,* pp. 286 ff., 306 ff.

The party gets its strength from the interests it represents, the convention and executive committee from the
party, and the chairman from the convention and committee. In each grade of this series the social fact actually
before us is leadership of some underlying interest or set
of interests.

To be sure, no informed sociologist would claim that
this position as to the nature of political parties is a novel
and unique contribution to the subject. It has been the
prevailing interpretation of the fundamental nature of
political parties by penetrating students of politics from
the time of Aristotle, and was particularly dominant
among the leaders of American political thought and
practice in the patristic period of John Adams, Hamilton,
Madison and Jefferson. What the sociologists can claim
is a large share in the current revival of this doctrine
and the more profound and elaborate analysis of this
proposition. While others have made notable contributions to this phase of sociological analysis, the real credit
for this departure must be assigned to Gumplowicz, Ratzenhofer, and Oppenheimer in Europe, and to their dis-
ciples and collaborators in this country, Small, Bentley,
and Ward. While there is no doubt that Gumplowicz
was the first of this group in respect to the priority of the
promulgation of the doctrine, the most thorough analysis
of political processes and parties as the social manifestation of the dynamic impulses coming from vital human
interests has been the work of Ratzenhofer. As Professor Small puts it: [34]

[34] Cf. his discussion of Giddings' paper on "Social Causation," in *Publications of the American Economic Association,*
third series, Vol. V, No. 2, p. 181. Cf. also Ratzenhofer, *So-*

We need to know, in the concrete, just how human interests have combined with each other in every variety of circumstances within human experience. There has never, to my knowledge, been a fairly successful attempt to schedule efficient human interests in general, till Ratzenhofer did it less than ten years ago in *Das Wesen und Zweck der Politik*. With this work sociology attained its majority. Henceforth all study of human relations must be rated as provincial, which calculates problems of life with reference to a less comprehensive scheme of interests than his analysis exhibits.

The linking up of this view of political parties with observed facts in party history and activity is easy when attention is concentrated on European parties or on most phases of American party history. The Fathers were perfectly frank in acknowledging that the early parties in this country represented an alignment of interests. In the last two decades, however, since the currency, tariff, and expansionist policies have ceased to divide the two old parties in this country, it is difficult for some to harmonize American party alignments with the theory of the party as an interest-group. Incisive publicists have, however, pointed out the fact that the task is not difficult when one goes beneath the superficial declamations of the party leaders and the party press. Both parties in this country are at present whole-hearted representatives of the capitalistic groups, and neither represents the agrarian or labor elements which for various special reasons have failed to develop a coherent party organization.[35] In

ziologie, "Vorwort," p. xii, for an acknowledgment of his indebtedness to Gumplowicz.

[35] Cf. Schlesinger, *New Viewpoints in American History,* Chap. XII; also Weyl, *The New Democracy.*

other words, real representative party government in this country has for the time being been suspended. Further, in the major parties there has been a distinct perversion of a means into an end. To the "organization" or "machine" elements the party has become an end in itself, and the income which it has received from the spoils and favors granted to it by the protected "vested interests" has made it worth conserving, and at the same time has made the party "ring" an interest-group of the most persistent and insidious sort.[36] As Bentley has summarized this matter, "the spoils system has operated to hold the party leaders from big to little together in a strong interest-group, which came, on the line of analysis I have previously set forth, to be more like an underlying interest-group than like a strict party formation on a representative level."[37]

As to the social function of political parties, viewed as contending interest-groups, sociologists are inclined to hold that party strife, in spite of all obvious selfishness and corruption, is one of the chief dynamic agencies in promoting political progress and stimulating a healthy political activity. In the same way that the physical conflict of social groups created the state and modern political institutions, so the more peaceful struggle of parties within the state secures the continuance of political evolution. In

[36] For an analysis of the perversion of representative government under the recent American party system, cf. Weyl, *The New Democracy;* Haworth, *America in Ferment;* Beard, *Contemporary American History;* Sumner, *The Challenge of Facts and Other Essays;* Small, *Between Eras: from Capitalism to Democracy;* Kales, *Unpopular Government;* Ross, *Changing America,* and *The Social Trend.*

[37] Op. cit., p. 415.

no healthy and progressive state can one expect a cessation of the conflict of interest-groups, though, as Novicow long ago pointed out, the highest form of conflict is that which is carried on in the psychic and cultural realms. This may ultimately be hoped to supersede the prevailing economic struggles of the present day, in the same way that the latter have generally replaced the lower biological contest of groups in the "state-making age." [38] Ward, with his striving for scientific analogies, has defined party strife as "social synergy"—a powerful creative force or principle; and he summarizes as follows his notion of the contributions of parties to political progress: [39]

> The vigorous interaction of the two forces, which looks so much like antagonism, strife and struggle, transforms force into energy and energy into power, and builds political and social structures. And after they are constructed, the same influences transform them, and it is this that constitutes social progress. Political institutions—the laws of every country—are the product of this political synergy, the crystallized action of legislative bodies created by political parties.

Next to the nature of political parties and their social function, the most important sociological problem is the explanation of the seemingly inevitable tendency of political parties to become oligarchical in their organization and to identify the party with the organization itself and the leaders in the organization. Giddings has suggested that

[38] Cf. Small, *General Sociology*, pp. 306 ff.; also Small's review of Ross' *Sin and Society*, in the *American Journal of Sociology*, Vol. XIII, pp. 566–8.

[39] "The Sociology of Political Parties," in the *American Journal of Sociology*, Vol. XIII, pp. 440–1. Cf. also Morse, *Political Parties and Party Leaders*, Chaps. I–III.

this is the result of the inevitable tendency of the few to dominate in all social organization and activity. Linking this up with his basic theory of social causation as differential response to stimulation, he finds that some react to new situations much more readily than others and, by their priority and resourcefulness, dominate all social situations. Oligarchy in parties, then, is a natural result of unlike or differential response to stimulation, and of the tendency in all organization to convert means into ends : [40]

Not all individuals react to a given stimulation with equal promptness, or completeness, or persistence. Therefore in every situation there are individuals that react more effectively than others do. They reinforce the original stimulation and play a major part in interstimulation. They initiate and take responsibility. They lead: they conduct experiments in a more or less systematic fashion.

Those individuals that react most effectively command the situation and create new situations to which other individuals must adjust themselves. Few or many, the alert and effective are a protocracy: a dominating plurum from which ruling classes are derived. Protocracy is always with us. We let George do it, and George to a greater or less extent "does" us.

Every kleptocracy of brigands or conquerors, every plutocracy, every aristocracy, and every democracy begins as a protocracy. It comes into existence and begins its career as a little band of alert and capable persons who see the situation, grasp the opportunity, and, in the expressive slang of our modern competitive life, "go to it" and with no unnecessary delay.

We have now arrived at the first induction, the funda-

[40] Giddings, "Pluralistic Behavior," loc. cit., p. 539; also, *The Responsible State,* p. 19.

mental principle of political science, which is, namely:
The few always dominate.

A number of the social psychologists have suggested
explanations for this oligarchical tendency of parties.
Sighele, LeBon, Tarde, Durkheim, and Ross have held
that it is due to the domination of the crowd psychology in
modern political assemblies and even in states as a whole,
where psychic contagion is induced by the operation of
the press and other agencies for expediting the spread of
information and the generation of uniform emotional
states. Under these circumstances the leaders can manipulate the masses at will and hold the situation completely
under their control.[41]

The technique through which party leaders dominate
the party and manipulate public opinion has been incisively
analyzed from the psychological standpoint by Wallas.
The important political entities which stimulate mankind
are not interpreted by the citizens as a complex of ideas
and desires, but only through the association of this political complex with some symbol. The most important
among the modern stimuli from the political order are
furnished by the political party. While a party may have
a conscious intellectual origin and be designed to achieve
a definite end, it will have little strength or endurance
unless it secures symbols with sufficiently high emotional
values, such as party colors, tunes, names, and the like. A

[41] Cf. Sighele, *Psychologie des sectes; La foule criminelle;*
Le Bon, *The Crowd; La psychologie politique;* and *The Psychol-
ogy of Socialism;* Tarde, *Les transformations du pouvoir;
L'opinion et la foule;* and *Les crimes des foules;* Durkheim, *Les
règles de la méthode sociologique;* Ross, *Social Control;* and
Social Psychology.

skillful party makes use of its symbols in the same way that a commercial concern employs its trademarks and advertisements. If a candidate is not properly surrounded by and vested with symbols, he has no chance of success. The most insignificant non-entity properly associated with the party symbols is much more likely to be successful in an election than the strongest personality in the country if he has cut himself off from party connections and makes a direct appeal to the intelligence and good judgment of the citizens. In this way the public is put at the mercy of the political organization, and the latter soon comes to regard the party as an end in itself or as a means for advancing the interests of the machine. The only avenue of escape from party tyranny lies in a removal of the psychological power of party symbols and in a discrediting of the political "spell-binder" through some method of revealing to the people the manner in which they are being exploited through set phrases and emotion-charged symbols. Such a procedure might operate as a political therapeutic.[42]

A remarkable sociological synthesis of the causes for the universal development of oligarchical tendencies in political parties is furnished in the monumental sociological analysis of political parties by the Swiss professor, Robert Michels.[43] He finds that oligarchical tendencies are inevitable in all forms of political organization and in all parties, even though the political organization be that

[42] Cf. Wallas, *Human Nature in Politics*, pp. 54, 72–186.—An even more acute analysis of symbolism in modern democracy and party activity is contained in Lippmann's *Public Opinion*, Chaps. XIII-XIV.

[43] *Political Parties: a Sociological Study of the Oligarchical Tendencies of Modern Democracies.*

extreme form of decentralization known as syndicalism or the parties be radical revolutionary parties. He finds that there are three chief causes for this situation: the psychology of the individual; the psychological characteristics of groups and mass government; and the inevitable accompaniments of organization. The average individual is stupid and lacking in initiative and resourcefulness. The more alert and intelligent naturally come to the top as leaders; but the psychological consequences of leadership are vanity, arrogance, impatience of popular control and a tendency to forget that they owe their position to popular consent. Under modern conditions democracy, in a broad sense, is mass rule. But masses are incoherent and inarticulate; they must have leaders. Further, the masses cannot participate directly in government; they must choose representatives, and representative government means organization. Wherever the masses do act in modern politics they are subject to the crowd-psychological state. In elections they are easily manipulated. The press, which is under the control of the leaders, can easily deceive them. Even modern parliaments, made up of chosen representatives, operate under psychological conditions very similar to the crowd. They are so large and unwieldy that they inevitably come under the domination of the able minority. But the great cause of oligarchy in political parties comes from the necessity of organization. It is the inevitable organization which a political party must undertake, if it is to function effectively, which produces the necessity of leadership and the consequent development of oligarchy. In the light of present experience and past history one is safe in concluding that democracy is much more likely to

be a healthy aspiration than a successful realization.   The
following rearranged excerpts from Michels' treatise
summarize his position in a fairly adequate manner: [44]

Democracy is inconceivable without organization.   Yet
this politically necessary principle of organization, while it
overcomes that disorganization of forces which would be
favorable· to the adversary, brings other dangers in its
train.   We escape Scylla only to dash ourselves on Charyb-
dis.   Organization is, in fact, the source from which the
conservative currents flow over the plain of democracy, oc-
casioning there disastrous floods and rendering the plain
unrecognizable.   It is obvious that such a gigantic number
of persons belonging to a unitary organization cannot do
any practical work upon a system of direct discussion.
Hence the need for delegation, for the system in which
delegates represent the mass and carry out its will.   Even
in groups sincerely animated with the democratic spirit,
current business, the preparation and the carrying out of the
most important actions, is necessarily left in the hands of
individuals.   Organization implies the tendency to oligarchy.
In every organization, whether it be a political party, a
professional union, or any other association of the kind,
the aristocratic tendency manifests itself very clearly.   The
mechanism of the organization, while conferring a solidity
of structure, induces serious changes in the organized mass,
completely inverting the respective position of the leaders
and the led.   As a result of organization, every party or
professional union becomes divided into a minority of di-
rectors and a majority of directed.   Every solidly constructed organization, whether it be a democratic state, a

[44] Op. cit., pp. 21, 22, 26, 27, 31, 32, 35, 130, 135, 230, 401, 405.
While the above summary and the following excerpts summarize the author's chief theoretical propositions, they give no adequate impression of the subtle analysis and the large amount
of concrete illustrative material contained in what is the most
important sociological contribution to the study of political
parties

political party, or a league of proletarians for the resistance of economic oppression, presents a soil eminently favorable for the differentiation of organs and functions. The technical specialization that inevitably results from all extensive organization renders necessary what is called expert leadership. Consequently the power of determination comes to be considered one of the specific attributes of leadership, and is gradually withdrawn from the masses to be concentrated in the hands of the leaders alone. Thus the leaders, who were at first no more than the executive organs of the collective will, soon emancipate themselves from the mass and become independent of its control. It is indisputable that the oligarchical and bureaucratic tendencies of party organization is a matter of technical and practical necessity. It is the inevitable product of the varied principle of organization. The press constitutes a potent instrument for the conquest, the preservation, and the consolidation of power on the part of the leaders. The press is the most suitable means of diffusing the fame of the individual leaders among the masses, for popularizing their names. In all cases the press remains in the hands of the leaders and is never controlled by the rank and file. When in any organization the oligarchy has attained an advanced stage of development, the leaders begin to identify with themselves, not merely the party institutions, but even the party property, this phenomenon being common both to the party and to the state. Reduced to its most concise expression, the fundamental sociological law of political parties may be formulated in the following terms: "It is organization which gives birth to the dominion of the elected over the electors, of the mandataries over the mandators, of the delegates over the delegators. Who says organization, says oligarchy." The treasure in the fable may well symbolize democracy. Democracy is a treasure which no one will ever discover by deliberate search. But in continuing our search, in laboring indefatigably to discover the indiscoverable, we shall perform a work which will have fertile results in the democratic sense.

CHAPTER VIII

SOCIOLOGICAL THEORIES OF SOVEREIGNTY, LIBERTY AND RIGHTS

1. *The Sociological View of Sovereignty*

The most important contributions which sociologists have made to the subject of political sovereignty have been in the way of indirect discussions, through a tracing of the genesis of social and political organization, the sketching of the social foundations of political control, and the analysis of the social and psychological basis of political obedience, rather than through a specific analysis of the concept of political sovereignty. Such contributions to the subject will, however, be reserved for the chapter dealing with extra-legal phases of political control.

A number of sociologists have denied the validity of the concept of absolute political sovereignty. Spencer, confusing somewhat the abstract conception of sovereignty with the notion of the absolute supremacy of a specific ruler or government, denounced the views of Hobbes, Bentham, and Austin. "Analyze his assumption, and the doctrine of Austin proves to have no better basis than that of Hobbes. In the absence of admitted divine descent or appointment, neither single-headed ruler nor many-headed ruler can produce such credentials as the claim to unlimited sovereignty implies." [1]   Bentley, with his desire to reduce the "raw material of politics" to a study of men and groups in action in concrete situations, is caustic in his criticism of the abstract notion of sovereignty: [2]

Sovereignty has its very important place in arguments in defense of an existing government, or in verbal assaults on a government in the name of the populace or of some other pretender, or in fine-spun legal expositions of what is about to be done.   But as soon as it gets out of the pages of the law-book or the political pamphlet, it is a piteous, threadbare joke.   So long as there is plenty of firm earth under foot there is no advantage in trying to sail the clouds in a cartoonist's airship.

Novicow and De Greef, looking at sociological problems from the standpoint of writers chiefly interested in international relations and an elimination of war through world federation, hold that the doctrine of absolute sovereignty cannot stand for a moment in the face of the observed facts of international interdependence, treaties, alliances, conventions, and concessions.   Its existence in fact and practice would bring about complete international anarchy. [3]

Other sociologists, while not rejecting entirely the importance or validity of the concept of sovereignty, have shown how far the metaphysical and juristic views must

[1] *Man versus the State,* ed. 1902, pp. 380–1.

[2] Op. cit., p. 264.

[3] Novicow, *Les luttes entre sociétés humaines,* pp. 534–5, 576, 626; *La politique internationale,* p. 97; *La critique du Darwinism social,* pp. 117, 296; De Greef, *La structure générale des sociétés.*

be modified in the light of a more scientific sociological analysis of social and political processes. One of the better known examples of this tendency is Giddings' sociological restatement of the doctrine of political sovereignty.[4] Analyzing in detail the metaphysical and juristic claim that there exists in every state "an original, independent, universal and irresistible power to compel obedience," he concludes that in human society no power can exist which possesses to a complete degree any one of these attributes, to say nothing of all of them. All are relative and subject to variations in social and political circumstances. The most extreme statement of the doctrine of sovereignty which can have any validity is that sovereignty is "the dominant human power, individual and pluralistic, in a politically organized and politically independent population."[5] The real nature of sovereignty can be understood only on the basis of an evolutionary sociological analysis:[6]

Let us pass now from these conceptions of sovereignty to the social fact of sovereignty; and let us ask whether we are justified in assuming that the fact has at all times been one and the same fact, or whether sovereignty itself may have been a variable, an evolutionary, phenomenon, created by and in turn creating varying moods of human feelings, varying attitudes of will, and consequently varying conceptions and speculations. This is a question which, I suspect, the student of political science as such or the jurist as such may be unable to answer. It is, I venture to

[4] Giddings, *The Responsible State*, pp. 36–47.
[5] Ibid., p. 48.
[6] Giddings, "Sovereignty and Government" in *Political Science Quarterly*, Vol. XXI, p. 7.

think, a sociological question; and I believe that the answer
to it, if found at all, must be found through ways of looking
at social facts and processes that are acquired only through
some sociological training.

After examining the evolution of sovereignty and the
various forms in which the power to secure obedience
has appeared, Giddings holds that one may distinguish
personal sovereignty, the sovereignty of a superior class
which may gain its power through social, economic or
religious prestige, the mass sovereignty of unlimited majority rule, and the domination of collective opinion and a collective will to which the public defers.[7] There are thus
four modes of sovereignty which are, broadly speaking,
chronological stages representing social and political progress: [8]

Of four possible and familiar modes of that superior
power which in political society actually secures the obedience of most men most of the time, one only is a power to
compel obedience, and that one is a power that is condi-
tional upon an obsession of the multitude. Personal sovereignty, the oldest and on the whole the commonest form,
is not a power to compel, it is rather a power to command
obedience. Class sovereignty, appealing through religion
and tradition to human sentiment, or relying on superior
wealth, is a power to inspire or to exact obedience. Mass
sovereignty, the sovereignty of the overwrought and emo-
tionally solidified multitude, is for the time being a true
power to compel obedience, since, while it lasts and as far as
it can reach, it is irresistible. And finally, the general sovereignty of an enlightened people that arrives at concerted

[7] Ibid., pp. 10–12.
[8] Ibid., p. 12.

130   Sociology and Political Theory

volition through reason and discussion is a power, through its appeal to intelligence, to call forth, that is to say, to evoke obedience.

These four modes of sovereignty do not come to exist by arbitrary chance without relation to the social environment. They are definitely correlated with types or phases of the social mind, which may be regarded as stages of social evolution. Personal sovereignty implies a predominantly ideo-motor population; class sovereignty is associated with sympathetic like-mindedness; mass sovereignty is a product of dogmatic like-mindedness; general sovereignty of the collective opinion and will is correlated with rational like-mindedness.[9]

A position similar to that of Giddings is taken by Ludwig Stein,[10] who contends that the principle of authority is as important for society as the principle of self-preservation is for the individual. In the course of the changes in the nature and source of authority, institutions have replaced persons as the source of authority. Originally, authority was imposed by individuals upon the community; now the community controls individuals. Formerly, authority was wielded for the benefit of the ruling classes, whereas at present it is consciously applied by the com-

[9] Ibid., pp. 12–13.—For an explanation of these types of like-mindedness, cf. Giddings, *Inductive Sociology*, pp. 133 ff.; and *Historical and Descriptive Sociology*, pp. 332 ff.

[10] "Autorität, ihr Ursprung, ihre Begrundung und ihre Grenzen," in Schmoller's *Jahrbuch für Gesetzgebung, Verwaltung, und Volkswirtschaft im deutschen Reich, 1902;* also "Die Träger der Autorität," in *Archiv für Rechts—und Wirtschaftsphilosophie,* Oct., 1907.—The essential doctrine of these articles is reproduced in his *Philosophische Strömungen der Gegenwart,* Chap. XV. His latest analysis is to be found in the *Einführung in die Soziologie,* pp. 388 ff.; and in *Die soziale Frage,* pp. 460 ff.

munity for the purpose of securing social discipline and the advancement of welfare of the group. The type of social authority depends upon the stage of civilization and the character and composition of the group. Force is the basis of the earliest source of authority. This is replaced by faith and credulity. In recent times a higher type of foundation has been found for authority in the domination of intelligence. The sources and organs of authority have been successively the elders, the shamans or medicine-men, the priesthood, the royalty, the military cult and the political bureaucracy, the lawyers, the academicians and scientists.

Commons has sketched a sociological theory of sovereignty which lays more stress upon the economic factors in society and politics.[11] He points out the various legitimate but differing approaches to the problem of sovereignty: the philosopher seeks the fundamental and universal basis of sovereignty and the ultimate foundation of the state; the lawyer is interested merely in locating the ultimate human authority over litigants; the political scientist is concerned with the nature, location, and results of sovereignty; the sociologist approaches the subject by analyzing the development of sovereignty and the state in their joint evolution as a product of social forces. He bases his conclusions on a concrete observation of man and society, and does not concern himself with the ultimate aim of the state or the universal philosophical justification of sovereignty. Sovereignty begins in private property. "Private property is but another name for that coercive relation existing between human beings through

[11] "A Sociological View of Sovereignty," in *American Journal of Sociology,* Vol. V, pp. 1–3.

which the proprietor commands the services of others.
This is also sovereignty." [12]   In fact, the state and all social
institutions had their origin in private property.[13]   There
are three basic constituent elements in sovereignty—coercion, order, and right.[14]   Coercion is "a means of com-
manding and securing for consumption the services of
others."   It rests upon some type of sanction, which is
"any expectation suggested by one person adequate to
arouse in another person motives leading to acts of service."   There are some five chief types of sanction which
may be arranged in the order of the decline of coercive-
ness and the development of persuasiveness.   These are
corporeal or the expectation of bodily punishment, priva-
tive or the expectation of the dispossession of property or
occupation, remuneratory or the expectation of material
rewards, reprobatory or the expectation of social penalties,
approbatory or the expectation of social rewards.[15]   One
of the main ethical and political problems of the state
is how much coercive power should be allowed to
private persons or classes in the promotion of their interests.[16]   Though sovereignty may originate in coercion, there can be no true sovereignty of the state
until order has been introduced through the establishment of constitutional restraints upon arbitrary despotism.[17]   Sovereignty is not original, as it is derived from
private property.   In the Middle Ages both were described by the same word, "dominion."   Sovereignty is

[12] Ibid., Vol. VI, p. 87.
[13] Ibid., Vol. V, pp. 13–14; Vol. VI, p. 88.
[14] Ibid., Vol. V, p. 350.
[15] Ibid., Vol. V, pp. 159 ff.
[16] Ibid., Vol. VI, pp. 81–2.
[17] Ibid., Vol. V, pp. 356 ff.

not absolute, unlimited or universal, for it is limited by
the coercion which still remains in private hands.[18]   "Be-
sides reducing coercion to order, sovereignty also squares
with right." [19]   Commons summarizes his theory of sovereignty as follows: [20]

Society precedes the state just as it precedes the family,
the church, the corporation, the political party. It unites
all of these as a tree unites its branches.

The state is the coercive institution of society. It is not
an ideal entity superimposed on society, but is an accumulated series of compromises between social classes, each
seeking to secure for itself control over the coercive elements which exist implicitly in society with the institution
of private property. Sovereignty is built up gradually by
a transfer of coercive power from private property to social
organization.

We have three constituents of sovereignty—coercion,
order and right. Coercion originates as private property.
The struggle for existence causes this to survive in the form
of monopoly and centralization. Order emerges as a constituent of sovereignty in place of caprice only when
sovereignty has extended over wide areas and when subordinate classes have earned the veto power in determining
the sovereign will. Right takes its place as the moral aim
of sovereignty when freedom has displaced material and
competitive necessity.

A more extreme doctrine of the economic basis and
determination of sovereignty and political institutions is
that put forward by the Italian writer, Achille Loria.[21]
He admits the similarity of his doctrine to Harrington's

18 Ibid., Vol. V, p. 365; Vol. VI, pp. 87–8.
19 Ibid., Vol. V, pp. 544 ff.
20 Ibid., pp. 3, 359, 552, 824.
21 *Economic Foundations of Society.*

theory that political power follows economic power. Present day society is generally divided into two general classes, the possessors of wealth and the dispossessed wage-earners.[22]

If we examine attentively the societies developing at the present day in the civilised countries of the old and new worlds, they present, we find, one common phenomenon: absolutely and irrevocably all of them fall into two distinct and separate classes; one class accumulates in utter idleness enormous and ever increasing revenues, the other, far more numerous, labors life-long for miserable wages; one class lives without working, the other works without living.

The chief economic basis of capitalistic domination is the ability possessed by the ruling economic classes to exclude the laborers from access to free land, thus keeping them at the mercy of the wage-system.[23] Yet, to assure themselves the safe perpetuation of this system of exploitation, the capitalistic class must secure control of certain "connective institutions," which will give them a dominating influence in nearly every phase of social life. The foremost of these "connective institutions" are morality, law, and politics: [24]

In order to support itself, capitalistic property must furthermore have recourse to a series of, what we may call, *connective institutions,* whose special function it is to guaran-

[22] Ibid., p. 1.

[23] Ibid., pp. 5–6.

[24] Ibid., p. 9; cf. also p. 380.—Even so cautious and scholarly a writer as Professor Seligman admits with respect to Loria's work that "on the whole we may affirm that the first thesis—the economic basis of the social constitution—has been adequately proven."

tee property against all reaction on the part of those excluded from the possession of the soil. The most important of these so-called connective institutions are: *morality, law* and *politics*. These great social phenomena may, accordingly, be regarded as organic products of capitalistic property—or property, at least, metamorphoses, and adapts them to suit its own ends. This is the point we have to prove.

In capitalistic society the economic system of exploitation and exclusion leads to a corresponding type of morality. Among the capitalists, morality, dictated by economic interest, prevents such a degree of exploitation as would lead to a revolt of laborers; and the laborers are trained by habit to act in obedience to the upper classes. Moral revolutions are but the reflection of an accompanying change in economic institutions.[25] A vital aid to the development and maintenance of this capitalistic morality arises from the fact that the capitalistic group is able to enlist the powerful assistance of the professional classes. The capitalists secure the support of the "unproductive laborers," namely, the artists, lawyers, physicians, journalists, and professors, by direct or indirect remuneration and favoritism. These professional classes, which have thus far been the chief molders of the ideas, opinions, and sentiments of the lower classes, convey the impression to the laborers that subjection is better than revolution, and try to convince them that there is a moral sanction for the existing social hierarchy and economic exploitation, thus "pulling the wool over the eyes of labor" and helping to offset the numerical weakness of the capitalists.[26]

[25] Ibid., pp. 21–2, 44, 51, 54, 68–9.
[26] Ibid., pp. 19–20, 160, 361.

Law is nothing but the juridical sanction which the ruling economic class give to existing economic conditions. "Legal history shows us that instead of being the product of abstract reason, or the result of national consciousness, or a social characteristic, the law is simply the necessary outcome of economic conditions." [27] Likewise, political sovereignty is but the ultimate force or power which maintains the capitalists in their exploitation. The state began in the association of laborers in a cooperative régime—and here the state and society were nearly identical. With the growth of private property, the territorial state superseded the tribal organization; with the concentration of private property in the hands of the capitalist class, the state became sharply differentiated from society and represented the interests of but a fraction of the total group of citizens. This led to a net increase of the power of the state, decreasing its pressure on capitalists and increasing tremendously its operation on the exploited. "Henceforth the state no longer echoed the peaceful and equitable expressions of universal consent, but became in the hands of a rapacious minority a terrible engine of defensive and offensive warfare against the exploited majority." [28] The type and distribution of economic revenue in society determines the nature of the political constitution, the form of the state, and the location of sovereignty. "Economic revenue stands in the same relation to political power as a principal to his agent, or a workman to his tool." [29] The division of revenue in society also determines the form of government and the

[27] Ibid., pp. 73, 79, 86, 114.
[28] Ibid., pp. 119 ff.
[29] Ibid., pp. 119, 135 ff., 141, 153 ff., 289, 327.

party alignment. Further, political revolutions, like moral and legal revolutions, are but a product and reflection of changes in the sources or distribution of economic revenue.[30] One may, therefore, conclude that "all the non-economic factors running through the social system would seem to be ultimately derived from the underlying economic conditions which alone furnish an adequate explanation of their complicated mechanism." [31]

Another extremely suggestive sociological analysis of the nature and limitations of political sovereignty is contained in E. A. Ross's work on *Social Control,* in which the analysis proceeds from the psychological rather than the economic point of view. Agreeing that social psychology deals with both individual and social ascendency, Ross concentrates his attention in this volume on social ascendency, or the domination of society over the individual.[32] There are two chief phases of social ascendency: the non-rational and non-purposive social domination through mob-mind, convention, and fashion, which may be summarized as social influence; and the rational and consciously designed ascendency which he designates as *social control.* He further separates the instruments or agencies of social control into two fundamental groups. The first type, which he characterizes as *ethical,* are senti-

[30] Ibid., pp. 169–77, 289 ff., 320 ff.—For Loria's views on the economic aspects of the World War, cf. his *Aspetta sociali ed economici della guerra mondiale.*

[31] Ibid., p. 380. Cf. also his *La sintesi economica.* The same doctrine is of course upheld with somewhat different premises and implications by Gumplowicz in his *Rassenkampf* and *Grundriss der Sociologie,* as well as by Oppenheimer in his *The State.*

[32] *Social Control,* Preface.

mental rather than directly utilitarian, draw their force
from the primal moral feelings, and embrace public opinion, suggestion, personal ideals, social religion, art, and social valuations. The second variety, which he terms the
political, refers to a set of influences which are not necessarily rooted in ethical or moral feelings, but are usually
based on a deliberately chosen policy. They include
such forces as law, belief, ceremony, education, and
illusion.[33]

The major part of the work is devoted to an analysis
of the manner in which these different methods of social
control operate in society and of the circumstances determining which set will be most influential and effective in
any given society. In summarizing the laws governing
their mode of operation he contends that political types
of control, which become effective through fear and prej-
udice, will be preferred in a society in proportion as "the
population elements to be held together are antipathetic
and jarring; the subordination of the individual will and
welfare is required by the scheme of control; the social
constitution stereotypes differences of status; the differences in economic condition it consecrates are great and
cumulative; the parasitic relation is maintained between
races, classes, or sexes." On the other hand, "the mild,
enlightening and suasive" ethical instruments of social control will be chosen and relied upon in proportion as "the
population is homogeneous in race; its culture is uniform
and diffused; the social contacts between the elements in
the population are many and amicable; the total burden
of requirement laid upon the individual is light; and the
social constitution does not consecrate distinctions of sta-

[33] Ibid., Preface and pp. 411 ff.

tus or the parasitic relation, but conforms to common elementary notions of justice." In other words, the obvious generalization from Ross' analysis is that the more perfect and highly developed the type of society, the more important become the non-political types of social control.[34]

This brief sketch of typical sociological contributions to the analysis of sovereignty will suffice to establish the proposition that political sovereignty is not original, absolute, universal or unlimited, that political power of any sort is rarely supreme in any society, that it is derivative rather than original, arising from social, economic and psychic forces, that sovereignty cannot be studied as an isolated entity, but only in its social setting and in the light of the evolution of the state within society, and that sovereignty in its deeper significance is a sociological rather than a political or legal problem, however important the determination of the legal superior may be in concrete instances for juristic purposes.

2. *The Sociological Conception of Liberty*

Sociologists have made significant contributions to the analysis of the sources, nature, importance, advantages, and limitations of liberty. All except the few who have distinctly anarchistic sympathies are agreed that the perennial discussion of whether liberty can coexist with au-

[34] Ibid., pp. 411–12. Cf. also Giddings, "Social Self-Control," in *Political Science Quarterly,* Vol. XXIV, No. 4. Of course, a number of other sociologists have contributed to the psychological analysis of sovereignty, especially Tarde, with his theory of the alternative sovereignty of beliefs or desires; but Ross' discussion is by far the most synthetic and suggestive.

thority is largely academic and scholastic. They accept as axiomatic the view that there can be no assured liberty without authority, though they do not lapse into the obsession of some neo-Hegelian eulogists of the state and contend that all extensions of authority really mean an accompanying increase of liberty. Hobhouse and Giddings have adequately expressed the normal sociological position on this point. Hobhouse says: [35]

The function of State coercion is to override individual coercion, and, of course, coercion exercised by any association of individuals within the State. It is by this means that it maintains liberty of expression, security of person and property, genuine freedom of contract, the rights of public meeting and association, and finally its own power to carry out common objects undefeated by the recalcitrance of individual members.

Giddings arrives at the same general conclusion: [36]

If the individual actually enjoys a high degree of liberty, it is because the social mind permits him to do so. It is because the sovereign state creates for him immunities and protects him in the enjoyment of them. This is a truth of Sociology and of political science which the uneducated man always finds much difficulty in comprehending. It seems to him that his liberty is born with him; that it is a matter of inherent right, and subject wholly to his own will. This is because he fails to realize how resistless is the power of his fellow-men over all his activities, and even over his life itself, if they choose to put that power in operation. If, at any time, he is so unfortunate as to fall under their suspicion, to be taken by them when they have resolved themselves into an angry mob, and to discover

[35] *Liberalism*, pp. 146–7.
[36] *Elements of Sociology*, pp. 218–19.

that he is utterly helpless in their hands if they choose to deal with him by the methods of lynch law, he then realizes that his liberty is not the creature of his own will, and that the liberty which any man actually enjoys, he owes to the common feeling and common judgment of the community that individual liberty is, on the whole, a good thing for all.

Again, sociologists have pointed out the fact that, significant as the liberty which is created and protected by the state may be, the greater part of the restrictions upon individual freedom have little or no relation to political institutions, but come from the mass of customs, usages, and folkways which determine to so large a degree most phases of human behavior and conduct. In other words, the discussion of political or civil liberty touches but a small portion of the real field of individual liberty. Sumner, who has done more than any other writer to indicate the over-powering significance of the non-political types of restraint on individual freedom, has well summarized this important matter: [37]

The most important fact about the mores is their dominion over the individual. Arising he knows not whence or how, they meet his opening mind in earliest childhood, give him his outfit of ideas, faiths, and tastes, and lead him into prescribed mental processes. They bring to him codes of action, standards, and rules of ethics. They have a model of the man-as-he-should-be to which they mould him, in spite of himself and without his knowledge. If he submits and consents, he is taken up and may attain great success. If he resists and dissents, he is thrown out and may be trodden under foot.

[37] *Folkways*, pp. 173–4. Cf. also Trotter, *Instincts of the Herd in Peace and War*.

Even the range of civil liberty is determined by social factors—is a function of the social mind. This is equally true of the amount of liberty enjoyed under the normal conditions in a given society and of variations of liberty due to special circumstances. Giddings, in his analysis of the character and efficiency of social organization, has shown how liberty is a product of the special character of the social mind in any group at any given time, the social mind depending upon the nature of the population elements, and the population elements being determined chiefly by the type of geographical environment. He has formulated the two following laws of liberty which indicate the relation between freedom and social circumstances : [38]

(1) Social organization is coercive in those communities in which sympathetic and formal like-mindedness strongly predominate over rational like-mindedness. Conversely, social institutions are liberal, allowing the utmost freedom of thought and action to the individual only in those communities in which there is a high development of rational like-mindedness.

(2) The forms of social organization, whether political or other, in their relation to the individual, are necessarily coercive if, in their membership, there is great diversity of kind and great inequality. Conversely, institutions or other forms of social organization can be liberal, conceding the utmost freedom to the individual if, in the population, there is fraternity and, back of fraternity, an approximate mental and moral equality.

Likewise, temporary variations from the normal amount of liberty enjoyed by a given society arise from social

[38] *Elements of Sociology,* pp. 218–221. Cf. also his "Theory of Social Causation," loc. cit.; and Ross, op. cit., pp. 411 ff.

situations and conditions; they are a product of the social phase of "circumstantial pressure." Anything which produces or threatens to produce a crisis in a society will cause a tightening up of the agencies of social control and a more thorough regimentation of the group for unified and rapid action. Liberty must, under such circumstances, be temporarily curtailed in the interest of group strength and survival. Examples of such circumstances are, of course, the familiar ones of war, threatened invasion, great disasters, such as devastating fires, earthquakes, pestilence, famine, revolution and any other imminent danger to the whole group or any considerable portion of the group. The reverse of this is likewise true, namely, that in times of plenty, peace, and freedom from disturbing influences a large amount of latitude is given to the individual in his activities. Few repressive laws are enacted, and many which exist on the statute-books are laxly enforced. Thus liberty, social and political, is a function of general social circumstances, both those which are relatively permanent and uniform and those which are sporadic and variable.[39]

A positive theory of liberty has been recently set forth from a socio-psychic standpoint by Graham Wallas.[40] While liberty, by derivation, means a condition of freedom from all obstruction to our impulses, the feeling of unfreedom does not arise except when "the hindrance is felt to be inconsistent with those normal human relation-

---

[39] Giddings, "Pluralistic Behavior," loc. cit., esp. pp. 390–1, 540, 549. The detailed treatment of the social causes for variations in liberty will be found in Giddings' forthcoming work on statistical sociology. Cf. also his *Studies in the Theory of Human Society*, Preface and pp. 190–223.

[40] *Our Social Heritage*, Chap. VII

ships, to which, in the environment of primitive society, our instincts correspond." But we cannot expect to live wholly in harmony with our primitive impulses in modern society : [41]

No way of living, therefore, can now be so "natural" to us as never to involve the obstruction of impulse; the principle of Liberty can never be absolute, and in the organization of our society, we must ask, not merely how we are to prevent the occurrence of the feeling of unfreedom, but how we are to live the good life.

From this position he reasons that a constructive sociological theory of liberty must be more than the purely negative conception of Mill and others, namely, freedom from restraint. He finds that the Periclean conception of liberty is far superior to this negative Manchester version : [42]

To Pericles, Liberty is no longer the merely negative fact of the absence of foreign tyranny. It is a many-sided positive conception, both of a type of political and social organization already in part realized in Athens, and of the conscious moral and intellectual efforts which alone could make the continued existence of that type possible. . . .

No modern thinker has expressed, for the purposes of modern national democracy, a conception of Liberty approaching in psychological insight the ideal which Pericles offered to the ancient City-state.

Wallas' whole work is his own effort to present a positive plan for social cooperation which will conserve the essentials of social liberty dictated by social psychology.

Further, sociologists have contended that it is unsatis-

[41] Ibid., p. 165.
[42] Ibid., p. 166-8.

factory to analyze the problems of liberty without some discrimination as to the various possible types or modes of liberty and some exact understanding as to the particular type of liberty under discussion. Perhaps the most successful attempt along this line of differentiating the various types or phases of liberty and indicating the implications of each type has been that of L. T. Hobhouse.[43] He divides his analysis of liberty into the following phases: civil liberty, fiscal liberty, personal liberty, social liberty, economic liberty, domestic liberty, local, racial and national liberty, international liberty, and political liberty. He has thus been enabled to arrive at illuminating definitions and penetrating analysis and, at the same time, to attain preciseness of thought and specific delimitation.

Finally, on the basis of sociological analysis similar to the foregoing, sociologists have pointed out the futility, if not hypocrisy, of attempting to class a political group as a liberal state or to assert that a population has freedom merely on the basis of the formal constitutional or legal protection, immunities or rights possessed by the citizen. A citizen may be protected by the first ten amendments to the American constitution, and by analogous clauses in state constitutions, or by the English Bill of Rights and all subsequent English guarantees of liberty, and may be eligible by law to exercise the right of suffrage and to election to the highest office in the land, and yet be compelled to stand in the bread-line, may find it actually impossible to combine with his fellow men to advance his economic well-being, may discover that the

[43] *Liberalism, passim., esp.* Chap. II.

press is closed to his attempt to make public his griev-
ances, may learn that "justice and the poor" rarely co-
habit, may see himself and his family excluded from social
functions, and may find even the Church proclaiming his
misery and subordination but a sure manifestation of an
inscrutable Providence.[44] It is such a situation as this
which will be obviated by the acceptance of a conception
of liberty as broad and comprehensive as that proposed
by Hobhouse in his classification of the sociological phases
of liberty.

3. *Sociology and the Notion of Political Rights*

Especially interesting has been the sociological restatement of the doctrine of political rights, particularly "natural rights." The sociological view of political rights is
that they are the rules of the game in the social process
which are accepted and applied by the community through
constitutional and statutory laws.[45] Rights, viewed in
this sense, are not what ought to be, according to some
ethical standard, but what *is* here and now. In its most
extreme form this notion even denies the validity of the
concept of natural rights. One of the most explicit state-
ments of this opinion is that of the Austrian sociologist,
Gumplowicz: [46]

[44] Cf. Small, *Between Eras;* Hobhouse, *Democracy and Reaction,* p. 166; *Liberalism,* pp. 248–51; *Social Evolution and Political Theory,* Chap. VIII; Loria, *Economic Foundations of Society,* pp. 127–35, 158–59; Giddings, *Principles of Sociology,* pp.
354–6; Tawney, *The Acquisitive Society;* Weyl, *The New Democracy;* Webb, *Industrial Democracy;* Stein, *Einführung in die
Soziologie,* pp. 297–306, 320–33.

[45] Sumner, *Earth Hunger and Other Essays,* p. 83.

[46] *Outlines of Sociology,* pp. 148–50, 180–1.

The premise of "inalienable human rights" rests upon the most unreasonable self-deification of man and overestimation of the value of human life, and upon complete misconception of the only possible basis of the existence of the state. . . . Rights are not founded upon justice. On the contrary, justice is created only by the actual rights as they exist in the state. It is the simple abstraction of political rights and it stands and falls with them.

Many sociologists have dissented from so extreme a doctrine as this, which is associated to a considerable degree with *Machtpolitik*.[47]   While agreeing that rights are, for the time being, what *is* in any society, they feel that there is yet room for a sociological reconsideration and restatement of the doctrine of "natural rights." Giddings was, perhaps, the earliest to work out the sociological theory of natural rights, and he has given this doctrine its most explicit statement.   Rejecting the seventeenth and eighteenth century identification of the natural with the primitive, he shows how, in the view of the sociologist, the natural is that which is "in harmony with the conditions of existence," and that "the unnatural is on the way to dissolution or extinction." [48]   Natural rights are those independent spheres of individual action which the selective process has demonstrated to be advantageous, if not indispensable, to the most rapid evolution of social organization and to the assurance of the progress of the race.   It is obvious that legal and moral rights must harmonize with natural rights, thus under-

[47] Giddings, *The Responsible State,* pp. 59–61.
[48] Giddings, *Principles of Sociology,* pp. 418–19. This is a complete answer to Ford's charge that Giddings and other sociologists are attempting to revive a pre-evolutionary notion in their theory of natural rights.

stood, if they are to be permanent, desirable or beneficial: [49]

> The sociologist finds nowhere a social force that has not
> been evolved in a physical-organic process, or one which is
> not at every moment conditioned by physical facts. He sees
> in constant operation that marvellous product of individual
> wills, the collective or group will, in which Austin found
> the source of political sovereignty; but he sees also, what
> no jurist before Darwin's day could have seen, how inexor-
> ably the sovereign will is conditioned by natural selection.
> The group, like the individual, can will, but what it wills
> is determined by conditions that man did not create, and
> whether the group continues to will this or that depends
> on whether the thing willed conduces to social survival.
> It is in this truth that the sociologist discerns the essential
> significance of the much-befogged doctrine of natural rights.
> Natural rights, as the term was once understood, has gone
> to the limbo of outworn creeds; not so those natural norms
> of positive right that sociology is just beginning to disclose.
> Legal rights are rights sanctioned by the law-making power;
> moral rights are rules of right sanctioned by the conscience
> of the community; natural rights are socially necessary
> norms of right, enforced by natural selection in the sphere
> of social relations; and in the long run there can be neither
> legal nor moral rights that are not grounded in natural
> rights as thus defined.

In a more recent work Giddings has still further elaborated this point of view; having indicated the manner in
which natural rights gradually and unconsciously develop
as products of the essential and indispensable conditions
of group existence and evolution, he has insisted that
natural rights must be divided into two categories—the

[49] Ibid., p. 418

natural rights of the community no less than the natural rights of the individual: [50]

Habits of toleration are older than men, older than reason. They are products of ineffective conflict. Countless generations of group-dwelling animals, and innumerable generations of primitive men one after another learned that creatures of one kind are approximately equal in strength, while creatures of different kinds are unequal. Physical similarity carries with it approximate equality of power, and equality of power insures a measure of freedom from meddling by one's neighbors. Group-dwellers are not born free and, therefore, equal. They are born approximately equal and, therefore, acquire freedom. In the last analysis, toleration is a behavior habit expressive of an equilibrium of physical strength.

About toleration as a habit, ideas of immunity and liberty began to cluster as human intelligence developed. Men quarreled and settled their differences. Bystanders approved or disapproved, and slowly the fabric of custom grew. Dimly at first, and then more clearly, men saw that social cohesion is imperative if the group is to be strong in war, and they began to understand that immunities and liberties, preventative of internal strife, are necessary conditions of social cohesion. So, imperceptibly, I suppose, and with unimaginable slowness and difficulty, animal habits of toleration became human *mores,* or customs of immunity and liberty.

As mores they were entirely objective. The customary claims, immunities, and liberties of the individual not only were asserted by him; they were also consented to and confirmed by his fellows. They were not merely right; they were rights. In a word, they were "natural rights"— not instituted, not invented, but products of an unconscious growth and inheritance. Collectively, they were the stuff or content of natural justice. They held men together in

[50] *The Responsible State,* pp. 59–68.

effective social cohesion for ages before political organization came into being. They underlie political organization now. They are the moral foundations of the responsible state, which adapts itself to them and builds upon them.

Natural rights are of two categories. There are natural rights of the community, and natural rights of the individual. Both the community and the individual have a natural right to exist and a natural right to grow or develop.

If mankind or any moiety of the human race has a moral right to exist, a community or society has such a right because it is only through mutual aid that human life is possible, and only through social relationships that the intellectual and the moral life of man can be sustained. . . .

If society is to endure, individual growth is subject to imperative limitations. It must be a function of inhibitions no less than of spontaneous actions. Natural justice prescribes the limitations. The individual has a moral right, confirmed in natural rights, to develop on equal terms with fellow individuals. All have equal, but only equal rights to life, liberty, and the pursuit of happiness.

In like manner, if civilized human society is to survive and civilized man is to continue his career of progressive achievement, the growth of communities must proceed within the limitations set by natural justice.

A very similar position is taken by Hobhouse. Holding that natural rights are not, as was held by Locke, Paine, and Jefferson, something which exist independent of, and prior to, society, he contends that they involve those concessions to the individual which are indispensable to the most efficient functioning of society and the progressive development of the social organism: [51]

[51] *Social Evolution and Political Theory,* pp. 196–200; cf. also his *Liberalism,* pp. 54–60, 132–7.

Unless we are to suppose deep-seated conflict in the ethical order we must regard the common good as the foundation of all personal rights. If that is so, the rights of man are those expectations which the common good justify him in entertaining, and we may even admit that there are natural rights of man if we conceive the common good as resting upon certain elementary conditions affecting the life of society, which hold good whether people recognize them or not. Natural rights, in that case, are those expectations which it would be well for a society to guarantee to its members, whether it does or does not actually guarantee them. If this view is accorded, the more developed the conception of the common good the more completely will a society guarantee the natural rights of its individual members. To extend the conception of the rights of the individual will be one of the objects of statesmanship; to define and maintain the rights of its members will be the ever extending function of government.

Any genuine right then is one of the conditions of social welfare, and the conception of harmonious development suggests that there will be many such conditions governing the various sides of social life. . . . Now in general the problem of social philosophy is to define in principle, and of statesmanship to adjust in practice the bearing of these several conditions.

An interesting related view is that of Cooley. He examines the basic social or primary ideals of loyalty, truth, service, kindness, justice, and freedom; indicates the manner of their genesis in the face-to-face groups of the family, play-group, neighborhood, and community; and shows the difficulty which is met in attempting to extend the application of these socializing forces on a larger scale in the national state. He believes that natural rights flow from these primary ideals through which society has taken shape, and that the limitations imposed on the primary ideals in larger social aggregates correspond to the social contract: [52]

In its older form this doctrine of natural right is wholly at variance with evolutionary thought. To the latter, society is an organic growth; there is no individual apart from society, no freedom apart from organization, no social contract of the sort taught by these philosophers. In its practical applications, however, the teaching of natural right is not so absurd and obsolete as is sometimes imagined. If it is true that human nature is developed in primary groups which are everywhere much the same, and that there also springs from these a common idealism which institutions strive to express, we have a ground for somewhat the same conclusions as come from the theory of a natural freedom modified by contract. Natural freedom would correspond roughly to the ideals generated and partly realized in primary association, the social contract to the limitations these ideals encounter in seeking a larger expression.

Indeed, is it not true that the natural rights of this philosophy—the right to personal freedom, the right to labor, the right to property, the right to open competition—are ideals which in reality sprang then as they do now largely from what the philosophers knew of the activities of men in small, face-to-face groups?

The reluctance to give up ideals like those of the Declaration of Independence, without something equally simple and human to take their place, is healthy and need not look far for theoretical justification.

Wallas has recently suggested a discriminating, dynamic, and positive theory of natural rights. He differentiates what it is natural for us to claim in response to our native impulses, which were developed in a primitive en-

[52] *Social Organization,* Chap. IV, esp. pp. 46-8.

vironment, from what it is socially desirable for us to
have in our highly complex modern environment. What
our primitive nature may desire must be progressively
limited and compromised with what it is now socially
right for us to have: [53]

Natural Rights are real things, arising from real and permanent facts in our psychology. But because the instinct
which creates them was evolved to meet the needs of a primitive environment, we must remember that in our modern environment it is no more invariably good for us to receive all
our natural rights than it is to be completely free. It may be
better on any particular occasion to endure the pain involved
in the obstruction of the instincts which makes us claim our
rights; or to "sublimate" those instincts by satisfying them
in a new way; or even to inhibit them by an effort of will,
based on a calculation of results, and leading to a disciplined
but unstable habit. All of this may sound obvious enough;
but if one considers the use of the term Natural Right during
the centuries when it had its greatest driving force, one continually finds that confusion and bloodshed was caused by the
fact that there was no common ground between men who felt
a passionate instinctive desire for their Rights, and men
who demanded a rational explanation and delimitation of
them. . . .

Both the psychological and the metaphysical argument suffered from the fact that men have continually ignored the
difference between that which it is natural to us to claim,
and that which is, in view of the whole circumstances, good
for us to receive; if a claim is natural, men have assumed
that its satisfaction is good for us, and if its satisfaction is
good for us, they have assumed that the claim is natural.
One would say that they have played with two different
meanings of the word "right," if it were not that they have
never recognized that the two meanings are different.

[53] *Our Social Heritage,* pp. 187–90. Cf. also Stein, *Die soziale
Frage,* pp. 112 ff.; 503 ff.

CHAPTER IX

SOCIOLOGY AND THE SCOPE OF STATE ACTIVITY

1. *The Sociological Case for Individualism and Laissez-faire*

There has been no more persistent error and no more deplorable source of confusion than the identification of sociology with socialism and a program of extensive state activity.[1] As might be expected, sociology, like the other social sciences, has had representatives who have sponsored a program of thorough-going state activity approximating socialism, and others who have frankly recommended the abolition of the state and the placing of reliance upon the non-political principle of social coöperation. The great majority of sociological writings have been distributed somewhere between these extremes.

The only distinguished sociologist to stand out as an exponent of anarchism is the Russian writer, Prince Kropotkin. Affected, no doubt, by the communistic features of the Russian agrarian society and by the oppression, brutality and corruption of the Russian state, as afflicted by the two-fold disease of Czardom and bureau-

[1] For a curious survival of this error, cf. so recent an opinion as that given by Carver in his review of Ross' "Principles of Sociology," in *Quarterly Journal of Economics,* Vol. XXXV, pp. 139 ff.

cracy, Kropotkin has set forth an historical and analytical defense of anarchistic society, founded upon voluntary cooperation, and dispensing entirely with the political state.[2]

The borderland between anarchism and respectable individualism has been occupied by another Russian writer, Jacques Novicow. He was also affected by the unfavorable light in which the state would inevitably be viewed by an intelligent Russian of the last generation, but his point of view was different from that of Kropotkin. He looked at political problems from the standpoint of an internationalist and pacifist. His ideals were cultural autonomy for national groups, political federation of the European states and an abolition of all war. It was perfectly logical that he should regard the European national state of 1870 to 1914 as the most sinister enemy of these ideals. The national state repressed subject nationalities; its fantastic claim to absolute and unlimited sovereignty was an insuperable obstacle to any stable or effective international organization; and the national state threw upon the people the enormous burden of supporting militarism or navalism, and waged bloody, expensive and needless wars, or threatened the world with such wars.[3] It is not surprising, therefore, that Novicow was an ex-

[2] *Mutual Aid a Factor of Evolution;* and *Anarchism, its Philosophy and Ideal.*

[3] Novicow, *War and its Alleged Benefits; The Mechanism and Limits of Human Association;* and *La fédération de l'Europe.* —Curiously enough, while Novicow evidences a bitter hatred of one of the chief products of modern capitalism, the militaristic and aggressive national state, his economic and political philosophy is identical with that of Cobden and Bright, and of John A. Bingham, Mark Hanna, Judge Gary, and Fabian Franklin.

ponent of that uncompromising individualism which would limit the state to acting as a collective policeman, concerned solely with the protection of the persons and property of the citizens. The state should protect property from being stolen and should secure the enforcement of contracts, but should go no further in the economic field. In this type of activity individual initiative has always been more effective than state interference. The state is worse than impotent when it attempts to interfere in cultural affairs. Even the state control of education has only served to fix it in a deadly routine and to preserve the program of studies bequeathed by the Renaissance. The state should hold entirely aloof from religious matters. Religious persecutions have invariably reacted to the detriment of the persecutors and have increased the number of adherents to the persecuted cause. Neither should the government meddle with moral questions. Public opinion alone is an adequate agency for moral regulation and guidance. Finally, Novicow would take the control of family relations and marriage out of the hands of the state, would remove all social and political disabilities from women, and would endeavor to improve conjugal and family relations by making psychic attraction rather than legal sanctions the foundation of family life.[4]

Probably the most distinguished and the best known sociological exponent of political individualism was Herbert Spencer. A number of elements seem to have entered into the determination of his attitude. Personal ex-

[4] *Les luttes entre sociétés humaines,* pp. 206 ff., 277 ff., 335 ff., 353–5, 484, 494, 604; *Conscience et volonté sociales,* pp. 237–8; and *L'affranchisement de la femme,* Bks. II and IV.

periences doubtless played their part. He was dominated by older male relatives during his childhood and developed thereby an anti-authority complex which was intensified by his chronic neurasthenia. Then his individualism, like that of Nietzsche, may have been in part a philosophy of personal triumph over physical suffering and adversity.[5] In his early environment, also, there were many influences making for individualistic doctrine. His youth was spent amidst the flourishing of the physiocratic social mechanics in economic and political theory, which represented state activity as a dangerous, if not an impious and sacrilegious, interference with the beneficent natural order. Later, his acceptance of evolutionary philosophy led him to hold that social evolution, as well as cosmic and organic evolution, was a spontaneous process which human action could only divert or obstruct. The large number of semi-sentimental programs of social reform between 1840 and 1870 did not serve to allay his suspicions with respect to the evils of state interference. In his earliest important work, *Social Statics*, Spencer set forth his individualistic political philosophy and listed the activities from which the state should refrain. These included, roughly, all those things which now constitute the chief activities of modern states and which even few conservative statesmen would think of questioning as valid political enterprises. He elaborated this doctrine in a long series of books and articles, culminating in his *Man versus the State,* and *Justice.* Here he concludes that the sphere of government should be limited to the protection of property and person from domestic and foreign

[5] See his *Autobiography,* passim.

attack and to provision for the freedom and enforcement of contracts. In other words, the state should concern itself wholly with "negative regulation." [6]

The most distinguished American adherent to this doctrine of *laissez-faire* was William Graham Sumner, perhaps an even more vigorous, forceful and dogmatic writer on the subject than Spencer himself. Sumner's views seem to have been a product of his own striking and self-reliant personality, of a somewhat reverent study of Spencer's writings, and of some practical observation of political effort in the municipal politics of New Haven. In various essays, among them *What the Social Classes Owe to Each Other,* he vigorously championed the cause of individualism. His chief arguments were that the state neglects its legitimate duty of protecting life and property when it goes further; that the burdens of state activity crush out the important and self-respecting middle class, made up of the "forgotten man," in order to aid the inferior classes that have lost out in the struggle for existence; that history has proved the state to be relatively incompetent in other fields than that of protecting life and property; and that social evolution is an automatic process which legislation cannot hasten but may retard. Sumner's specific advice to social reformers was "mind your own business," and his theory of state activity was almost identical with that of Spencer.[7]

[6] Spencer's more important works on this subject not enumerated above are *Essays, Scientific, Political and Speculative;* and *The Study of Sociology.* Cf. *American Journal of Sociology,* Vol. XXVII, pp. 314–22.

[7] Cf. in addition to the *Social Classes,* the four volumes of collected essays edited by Sumner's disciple and successor, A. G. Keller.

Another interesting sociological criticism of state activity has come from two writers who oppose state interference for the reason that it seems to be associated with modern democracy and its tendencies toward secularism and state socialism. These assailants of state activity from the clerical and aristocratic point of view are Gustave Le Bon in France and W. H. Mallock in England. Firm believers in aristocracy, authoritative religion and individualism, they have vigorously attacked modern democracy and state socialism and have defended extreme individualism.[8] Hilaire Belloc has attacked the capitalistic and secular state from the standpoint of social Catholicism, and has proposed a clerical brand of near Gild Socialism.[9] Another critic of state socialism from the clerical point of view has been Frédéric Le Play. Profoundly impressed with the evils of modern industrialism and sympathetic with the working classes, Le Play chose to put his faith in the improved family-group rather than the state as the chief instrument of social reconstruction.[10] From his doctrines there has also grown up the theory and practice of "regionalism" as a type of social reform, especially among his British followers, Victor Branford and Patrick Geddes. Their program borders, however, on municipal socialism.[11]

[8] Le Bon, *The Psychology of Socialism;* and *La psychologie politique;* Mallock *Aristocracy and Evolution; The Limits of Pure Democracy;* and *A Critical Examination of Socialism.*
[9] *The Servile State.*
[10] *La réforme sociale en France; La organisation de la famille;* and *La constitution essentielle de l'humanité.*
[11] Geddes, *Cities in Evolution;* Geddes and Branford, *The Coming Polity.* Cf. also Swinny, "The Sociological Schools of Comte and Le Play," in *Sociological Review,* Vol. XIII, pp. 68–74; and *Indian Journal of Economics,* Vol. III.

2. The Sociological Defense of State Activity and Social Politics

At the opposite extreme from writers such as Novicow, Spencer, and Sumner are those who, such as Comte, Ward, Hobhouse, Schäffle, and Stein, favor an extensive program of state activity. Comte had laid the basis for the viewpoint of this group, for in his Positivist state, instructed by sociologist-priests, moralized by women, and governed by the socialized *bourgeoisie,* he had provided for a considerable scope of state activity in social improvement.[12] It was left, however, for Lester F. Ward, an American sociologist profoundly influenced by Comte, to furnish the most scientific and comprehensive sociological defense of state activity in social reform. Holding that achievement rather than structure was the chief object of sociological investigation and exposition, that genesis was less significant than telesis, and that man could by well-advised legislation consciously improve the social order and accelerate social progress, Ward expounded the philosophy of state activity with an eloquence and scientific precision equalled by no other writer of ancient or modern times. As scathing in his denunciation of present-day partisan and plutocratic governments as either Spencer or Sumner, he pointed out the error of these "misarchists" in assuming that political life and activity could never be improved or purified. There are, according to Ward, four legitimate functions of government: the restraint, protection, accommodation, and amel-

[12] *Principles of a Positive Polity,* esp. Vol. II. Cf. also *The Open Court,* Vol. XXXVI, pp. 414–22, 497–512.

ioration of society. The fourth function, that of the amelioration or conscious improvement of society, while the most important of all, has as yet been but slightly developed. Its ultimate adoption can take place only when, in the sociocratic régime of the future, government has become a science and is no longer maintained chiefly to protect vested interests or to give support to a mass of party parasites. When political activity is based on the laws of social science and legislators have become sociologists, the state may safely begin in real earnest the problem of social reconstruction. No limits can be assigned to its action save those which social science will dictate in particular cases to be determined by a statistical presentation of the facts involved.[18]

Essentially the same position has been taken by the leading English sociologist, Leonard T. Hobhouse. Agreeing with Ward in his theory of the teleological future of social evolution, he represents the sociological expression of the Neo-Liberalism of England that has produced between 1905 and 1914 more constructive social legislation than the combined product of the earlier English governments since the accession of the Tudor dynasty in 1485. While distinctly an exponent of extensive state activity, Hobhouse is a keenly scientific and discriminating advocate. He recognizes that no universal program of social legislation can be laid down which would apply equally well to all societies in all stages of social evolution. The only generalization that can be

---

13 Ward, *Psychic Factors of Civilization*, pp. 311–37; *Dynamic Sociology*, Vol. II, pp. 212–17, 231–50; *Pure Sociology*, pp. 568–9; *Glimpses of the Cosmos*, Vol. III, pp. 301–5; Vol. IV, pp. 64–71; Vol. V., pp. 38–66.

made is that a harmonious and organic social life is essential, and this implies the maximum of efficiency and energy on the part of all social classes. The state is justified in acting in the premises in so far as action to be effective must be universal in its application to a class or the whole society and must involve compulsion. This formula is the most general statement of the philosophy of state activity, and within the field thus marked out there can be no valid arguments against state interference.[14]

Sympathetic likewise with extensive state activity have been the German sociologists, who, along with many economists, were designated *Katheder-Socialisten,* and were normally members of the *Verein für Socialpolitik.* Of these the most distinguished sociologist was Albert Schäffle, who was led by the organic analogy into conclusions quite different from, and perhaps more logical than, those of Spencer. From the standpoint of biological sociology the state appeared to him as the supreme coordinating and controlling agency in society. As a practical statesman he did much to urge and guide Bismarck in the formulation and adoption of the elaborate social legislation of the German Empire.[15] Practically the same position is taken by the German philosopher and sociologist, Ludwig Stein. Sympathetic with the advanced social legislation of Switzerland and with the German state socialism, Stein favors a positive and constructive program of legislation by the state. He believes that

[14] Hobhouse, *Social Evolution and Political Theory,* pp. 155–6, 168–201; *Liberalism,* pp. 163–211; *Development and Purpose,* Introduction; and *The Elements of Social Justice.*

[15] Schäffle, *Bau und Leben des socialen Körpers,* Vol. II, pp. 427 ff.; *Abriss der Soziologie;* and *Quintessence of Socialism.*

have shown how cultural assimilation and international sympathy must precede any permanent and effective union of nations or international peace. This does not require complete identity of culture, but it does call for a sufficient similarity in essentials to permit of effective co-operation.[22] Finally, Veblen has called attention to the difficulties involved in developing amicable international relations so long as national policy is dominated by the modern capitalistic "patriot promoter" with his book-keeping economy at home and his imperialistic policies in international relations. The chief economic causes of international rivalry must be eliminated, neutralized, or internationalized.[23]

Perhaps the most important sociological discussion of the problems of internationalism in the light of the recent World War has been contributed by Hobhouse, who in the latter part of his *World in Conflict,* and again in the concluding chapter of his *Questions of War and Peace,* deals with the question of the necessary reconstruction of international relations which should follow the war, if there is to be any hope that the world will be henceforth free of such calamities as that of 1914–1918. He sees two alternatives facing the states of the world, a continuance of militarism, preparedness, involving more wars and the cumulative self-destruction of Western civilization, on the one hand, and the provision of "some orderly mode of governing the intercourse of nations," on the other.[24]

[22] Giddings, "The Bases of an Enduring Peace," in *International Conciliation Bulletin,* No. 113. Tenney, "Theories of Social Organization and the Problem of International Peace," in *Political Science Quarterly,* Vol. XXX, pp. 1–14.

[23] Veblen, *The Nature of Peace.*

[24] Hobhouse, *Questions of War and Peace,* pp. 183–6.

The old cosmopolitanism, based on humanitarianism and free trade, died with Cobden. There is no longer any hope of reviving cosmopolitanism; only an internationalism based upon the recognition of both the existence and the interdependence of national states can serve as an adequate foundation for the international relations of the future. Hobhouse regards as insufficient guarantees of future peace such proposed solutions as The Hague Tribunal and arbitration agreements, union against an aggressive state which violates international law, and the economic boycott of offenders against the law of nations. "I am forced, therefore," he says, "to the conclusion that we must either go further or not attempt to move at all, and I should agree with my friend, Mr. Hobson, that there is no formal guarantee of a permanent peace except in the formation of an international state." [25] Hobhouse believes that the most practicable method of erecting a world-state consists in developing a federation out of the existing Entente Alliance, then uniting this to a federation of neutrals, and finally taking in Germany, when it becomes certain that the pacifist element dominates that country.[26] The following paragraph briefly summarizes his plan:

I would look forward, then, to the conversion of the existing Alliance into a permanent League or Federation, with a regular constitution and definite functions, which should include some measure of control over the production of munitions of war. But from the outset I would contemplate the extension of the League by the free entry of new mem-

25 Ibid., pp. 193–9.
26 Ibid., pp. 214 ff.; *The World in Conflict,* pp. 88 ff.

bers. . . . This would at once transform it from an ordinary alliance into something approaching a world-federation.[27]

There is little doubt that the events and outcome of the Peace Conference at Paris, as well as subsequent Allied diplomacy, disillusioned Mr. Hobhouse, as it did so many other hopeful liberals, in the matter of the adaptability of the Entente Alliance to furnishing the foundation of a trustworthy and durable league of nations.   No one can doubt, however, that the moral collapse of the Conference substantiated rather than discredited Hobhouse's thesis that some kind of world-organization must be provided if peace is to endure longer than is necessary for the European nations to recover from the losses sustained in the present conflict.[28]

[27] *The World in Conflict*, p. 94.
[28] Wallas has presented the same point of view in his *Our Social Heritage*.   For an excellent summary of the obstacles to permanent peace, as they appear to a sociologist, see the articles by Hankins, "Is a Permanent Peace Possible?" in *Journal of Race Development*, Vol. VIII; and "Patriotism and Peace," *Journal of International Relations*, Vol. XII.

The most candid exposition of the improbability of securing any significant results from the present League of Nations, in the light of the post-War psychology of Europe, has been set forth in the editorials of *The Freeman*.

CHAPTER XII

1. *Individualism versus Social Absolutism*

Nowhere has sociology contributed more to political theory than in the analysis of the extra-legal or extra-constitutional phases of social control. The sharp differentiation between society and the state is the cardinal fact distinguishing the sociological approach to political problems, and it is but natural that the most fruitful phase of sociological analysis should be along the line of indicating the manner in which general social conditions and processes affect political life and activity.[1] The sociological contributions to the subject of extra-legal elements in or affecting politics have been in part described in the chapters dealing with the fundamental elements in the state, the nature of the political process, and the nature and activities of political parties. Likewise, the biological, geographical, economic, and psychological factors bearing upon politics have there been catalogued and briefly analyzed. It remains to point out the characteristic views of sociologists on such questions as the relative importance of the individual and society in social activities, the nature, genesis, and functions of public

[1] Ross' discussion of the types of non-political agencies of social control have been referred to above, pp. 137–9. Cf. his *Social Control,* pp. 411 ff.

opinion, and the sociological and political significance of education.

It is often assumed that the sociological view of history and politics is identical with social determinism.[2] This is scarcely an accurate position, for, as on most other questions, there is a distinct division of opinion among sociologists as to the relative influence of individual and social forces in society. The domination of social pressure over the individual, and his subordination to socially determined institutions and processes, has been maintained by Ward among systematic sociologists; by Sumner, Durkheim, and Trotter from the psychological students of society; by Keller, Jacoby, Bateson, and Conklin as representatives of biological sociology; by Gumplowicz and others of the school most interested in the conflict of social groups; and by Ratzel and other exponents of the anthropogeographical interpretation of society.[3] Of the opposite opinion are Galton, Pearson, Ammon, Vacher de Lapouge, Mallock, Ludovici and Le Play, who defend individual ascendency.[4]

The more general sociological position on this problem is, however, an eclectic and synthetic one. A number of thoughtful writers, approaching the subject from a socio-psychological point of view, have challenged the discussion by insisting that to view the problem as one of the individual versus society is to mistake the questions at issue and to misinterpret the problem. Society and the in-

[2] James, *The Will to Believe, and Other Essays in Popular Philosophy*, pp. 229 ff.; Burr, in *American Historical Reivew*, Vol. XXII, p. 269; *Publications of the American Economic Association*, Vol. V, No. 2, pp. 190 ff.

[3] Cf. works cited above, pp. 57–64.

[4] Cf. works cited above, pp. 58, 90–92.

dividual are indispensable complements each to the other; neither could exist without the other, and it is even difficult, if not impossible, to differentiate individual from social factors. This point of view has been most effectively urged by Baldwin, Cooley, Wundt, and Ellwood.[5] Perhaps no one has expressed this conception more lucidly or concisely than Baldwin: [6]

The traditional contrast between individual and collective interests is largely artificial and mistaken. The individual is a product of his social life, and society is an organization of such individuals. There is, on the whole, no general antagonism of interests. On the contrary, there is a concurrence and practical identity, at least in those great aspects of life which constitute the utilities of society, and motive the essential actions of men.

Society and the individual are not two entities, two forces acting separately, two enemies making forced and grudging concessions each to the other. On the contrary, they are the two sides of a growing organic whole, in which the welfare and advance of the one minister to the welfare and progress of the other.

Another group of writers have attempted to state the situation by holding that, though social factors create the general institutional and cultural complex in which individuals function, yet the ablest and most alert individuals will assume the leadership and dominate the mass. Giddings has explained this on the basis of his theories of differential response to stimulation, pluralistic behavior

[5] Baldwin, *The Individual and Society;* Cooley, *Human Nature and the Social Order;* Wundt, *Elements of Folk Psychology;* Ellwood, *Sociology in its Psychological Aspects,* pp. 268 ff.

[6] Op. cit., pp. 118, 170.   Cf. also Cooley, *Social Organization,* Chaps. I-II.

and "protocracy." [7] Tarde, Ross and Baldwin have shown how the individual is the source of the inventions which are the cause of all social innovations and are disseminated through society by the process of imitation.[8] Michels has shown how the necessity of organization in modern society naturally throws the power into the hands of the most ambitious and capable leaders.[9] Stein has emphasized the essential nature of authoritative control in society and politics.[10] Le Bon has described in detail the manner in which the leaders of society are able to manipulate crowds and exploit the crowd-psychological conditions in modern society for their own advancement and selfish interests.[11] Comte, Ward and Wallas have indicated the importance of the individual in social invention along the line of securing rational control and direction of the social process.[12] Finally, an important contribution to the subject has been made by the anthropological and historical sociologists, who have indicated that the problem must be looked upon in a genetic manner. While the powerful chieftain or priest has a greater range for his ascendency in primitive society, it is unquestionably true that the potentialities for individual initiative and freedom increase with the evolution of society.[13]

[7] *The Responsible State,* pp. 17–20; also his "Pluralistic Behavior," loc. cit.

[8] Cf. works cited above.

[9] *Political Parties.*

[10] "Autorität, ihr Ursprung, ihre Begrundung, und ihre Grenzen," loc. cit., pp. 1–30.

[11] *The Crowd.*

[12] Comte, *Principles of a Positive Polity,* Vol. II, pp. 224 ff.; 286 ff.; Vol. IV, pp. 222 ff.; Ward, *Applied Sociology;* Wallas, *Our Social Heritage.*

[13] Cf. works of Boas, Goldenweiser, Lowie, and Wissler.

2. *Sociological View of Public Opinion*

Particularly important among the extra-legal forces in government is public opinion, especially so in the era of democracies.[14] This has been studied in detail by psychological sociologists. They have shown, in the first place, that the formation of public opinion is a socio-psychic process. Public opinion is produced, not by the adding together of individual opinions, but by the inter-action of the individual minds in a community. This interaction of minds follows certain laws of behavior and exhibits certain psychological processes which the psychological sociologists have analyzed. It is in this matter of describing the genesis and nature of public opinion that sociology has rendered the greatest aid to political scientists in this field of work.[15]

Giddings and McDougall have devoted a large amount of attention to the genesis, nature and operation of the social mind.[16] Their general analysis, as well as special contributions to the field from social psychologists, have for the first time made it possible to lay the foundation for a scientific study of the genesis of public opinion. Among the special contributions to the analysis of the factors entering into the shaping of public opinion may

[14] Bryce, *American Commonwealth,* Vol. II, Pt. IV.
[15] Cooley, *Social Organization,* pp. 107 ff.; Ross, *Social Control,* pp. 89 ff.; McDougall, *Group Mind,* Pt. I; Tarde, *L'opinion et la foule;* Giddings, *Inductive Sociology,* pp. III ff.
[16] Giddings, *Inductive Sociology,* Pt. II; McDougall, *The Group Mind.*

be mentioned Bagehot's analysis of the social and political function of discussion; Tarde's treatment of the diffusion of ideas and opinions through imitation; the discussion of the function of leaders by Cooley, Ross, Giddings, Le Bon, Michels, and others; the description of the operation of social impression and the crowd-psychological state by Durkheim, Trotter, Le Bon, Sighele, and others; Sumner's views as to the significance of custom and tradition in furnishing the content of public opinion, and Trotter's analysis of the manner in which herd instinct gives a vital impulse to the force of the mores; and the analysis by Ross and Wallas of the manner in which the vested social, economic, and political interests carry on a successful propaganda of deception by appealing to primitive and emotional impulses in the population through the use of symbols, shibboleths, catch-phrases, and other devices of the spell-binders and patrioteers.[17]

One of the most important phases of the sociological discussion of public opinion has been related to the question of the intellectual nature and level of public opinion, and its fitness as a guide for public procedure. Giddings, Cooley,[18] and McDougall [19] have maintained that public opinion is likely to be more rational, critical, and intelligent than individual opinions. Giddings, in fact, goes so

[17] The works of these writers dealing with these subjects have been cited in Chap. V.

[18] Giddings, *Inductive Sociology,* pp. 154-5; Cooley, *Social Organization,* pp. 121 ff.

[19] In his latest work on *The Group Mind,* pp. 28, 64 ff. In his *Social Psychology,* McDougall had expressed a distinctly less favorable view of public opinion.

far as to distinguish sharply between public opinion and popular opinions and beliefs, and defines public opinion as critically thought out social judgments.[20]   On the other hand, Spencer, Sumner, Trotter, Le Bon, Wallas, Tönnies, Lippmann, and others incline to the view that public opinion is likely to function on an emotional and instinctive level, that it is charged primarily with the old, traditional, customary and irrational psychic and cultural elements, and that it is scarcely fitted to assure critically determined conduct and progressive action.[21]

It would seem that the antagonism between the two groups of students of public opinion is less real than apparent; the former group of writers seemingly regard public opinion as it might be in an ideal or utopian society where the intellectual leaders controlled social opinion, and the latter look upon it as it actually exists under present conditions.

Much of the ablest critical discussion of public opinion which has yet appeared is contained in the recent work of Walter Lippmann.   Calling attention to the psychological difficulties encountered by the best intellects in grasping the facts and trends in our complex modern civilization, with its world-wide contacts, Lippmann demonstrates in a penetrating and convincing manner how pathetically inadequate are the processes of acquiring knowledge among the masses.   The background of their mental content and mode of acquiring information is to be found in tradition and habit.   Most concepts and categories for the reception and interpretation of new information are but "stereo-

[20] *Inductive Sociology.*
[21] Spencer, *Study of Sociology;* Wallas, *Human Nature in Politics;* and Tönnies, *Kritik der öffentliche Meinung.*

types"—illusory or defensive vestiges, chiefly from a more primitive layer of thought and culture. Giving evidence of the influence of his former teacher, Graham Wallas, Mr. Lippmann analyzes with acumen the dominant part played by symbolism in the thinking of the masses, and indicates how the possession of the symbols and other foundations for an emotional appeal gives the politicians and the dominant minorities an easy mastery over the uncritical majority. The masses have no preparation in the way of the possession of adequate facts or any training in scientific modes of thinking which would enable them to participate intelligently in the formation of a rational and informed public opinion. They are therefore readily controlled by the privileged few, who are masters of the art of mass manipulation. Perhaps the most original portions of Lippmann's work are his constructive proposals. It has been normally assumed that an objective and impartial press, pulpit, and lecture platform would be adequate to the creation and guidance of public opinion, but Mr. Lippmann abundantly proves that the complex problems of modern democracy require for their understanding and solution something far more scientific and expert than can be furnished by either press or pulpit, and he suggests an organization of expert fact-finding bureaus which will furnish the essential information upon which a rational public opinion and political education may be founded.[22]

Especially important, as bearing upon the nature and level of public opinion, are the studies by Veblen, Ross, Weyl, Lippmann and others of the various direct and indi-

[22] Lippmann, *Public Opinion;* cf. also his *Liberty and the News.*

rect methods of propaganda whereby the vested interests, through their control of politics, law, pulpit, education and press, set forth their own views and secure the acceptance of them by the public.[23]   In this way public opinion has become rather a bulwark of autocracy than a safeguard and servant of democracy.   Upon one point, however, there is practical unanimity of sociological judgment, namely, that the type and level of public opinion will be determined by general social conditions at large.   The degree to which public opinion will actually approximate rational and critical social judgment upon vital issues will depend upon such general conditions in the social population as homogeneity, social equality, education and literacy, objective search for facts and expert guidance, freedom of expression, possibility of publicity, and freedom in intercommunication.[24]

The most recent, and in many ways the most important, discussion that has been raised regarding public opinion is the question of its essentially monistic or pluralistic nature.   It has been conventionally assumed in sociological and political thinking, primarily as a result of Hegelian influences and the theory of the monistic state and absolute political sovereignty, that public opinion is something common to, and shared in by, all members of the community. The majority of the population has been assumed to have a vivid interest in matters of common concern and considerable unanimity of opinion upon these matters.   With

[23] Veblen, *Theory of the Leisure Class; The Higher Learning in America;* Ross, *Sin and Society; Changing America;* and *The Social Trend;* Weyl, *The New Democracy;* Sinclair, *The Brass Check;* Lippmann, *Preface to Politics; Liberty and the News;* and *Public Opinion.*

[24] Cf. esp. Lippmann, *Public Opinion.*

the progress of pluralistic doctrine in sociology, politics, and jurisprudence this position has been challenged. It has been contended that a man's thoughts will centre about the interests of his professional group or groups and that his opinions will be shaped largely by the views of the special and narrowly limited groups to which he belongs. One's views on matters of general import will necessarily be more vague and apathetic than his opinions on matters of immediate group concern, and, instead of uniformity of public opinion on the part of the social population, there will be a large number of divergent group opinions.

This line of thought goes back to Althusius' theory of the state and to Locke's essay on "The Law of Fashion and Private Censure." It has been developed from a psychological point of view by William James and Durkheim, and from economic, political and juristic premises by Gierke, Maitland, Duguit, Laski, and Cole. Cole and the Gild Socialists have attempted to save something from the wreckage of the older monistic view by contending that uniformity of opinion can be expected in matters concerning the interests of the population as consumers.[25] McDougall has expressed the opinion that in spite of this plurality of interests a man may participate in general public opinion through the building up a hierarchy of interests and opinions from his most intimate group concerns to those attachments which relate to the public at large.[26]

This review of sociological discussions of public opin-

[25] Cf. the references to the works of these writers cited above; also in Coker, "The Technique of the Pluralistic State," loc. cit.
[26] *The Group Mind*, pp. 115–19

ion will doubtless convince most readers that the subject is one which has just begun to be studied by scientific methods and that it is not likely to be greatly advanced except by socio-psychological investigation.

3. *Sociological Views of the Function of Education*

A significant and pertinent contribution of sociology to the non-political phases of social control is that relating to the function of education in social organization and progress. It is obvious that if the findings of social science are to have other than academic and esoteric significance, they must be disseminated among the members of the population, something which can be achieved only by a properly socialized system of education. Education from the sociological viewpoint is particularly significant in its relation to artificially directed social progress. To be effective, such a system of education must assume at the outset as basic premises the validity of the concept of progress and the possibility of achieving it artificially by social effort. It must inculcate those facts and principles which sociologists have agreed are indispensable to progress. It must also go further and indicate the agencies through which this advancement may be achieved, and aid in perfecting these instrumentalities of progressive growth.[27] This notion of socialized education as the indispensable prerequisite for progress was developed by Comte,[28] but it was reserved for Ward to make the subject almost his

[27] Cf. Ellwood, *Sociology and Modern Social Problems,* Chap. XVI.
[28] *Principles of a Positive Polity,* Vol. II.

own through the vigor and clarity of his treatment of it in his *Dynamic Sociology.*[29]

While it is necessary to recognize this dynamic function of scientific education, it is also essential to bear in mind that education in the past and at the present time is far less devoted to inculcating the information necessary for securing social progress than to handing down tradition, inspiring a love for the past, eulogizing the *status quo* in social institutions, and uttering warnings against the very idea of progress, while protesting its impossibility. There is much truth in Dr. Kallen's statement that "institutional education is a distraction from life, not a preparation for it."[30] Sumner, Chapin, Keller, Veblen, Sinclair, Robinson, Dewey and others have analyzed education from this standpoint and have shown how little we have to hope for from conventional educational methods in the way of promoting progressive advances in culture and social institutions.[31]

[29] Vol. II, Chaps. X-XIV; cf. also his *Applied Sociology,* Chaps. VIII–XII. Cf. references in Ellwood, op. cit., p. 387.

[30] An excellent presentation of the conventional non-social point of view on education and progress is to be found in Shafer, *Progress and Science.*

[31] Sumner, *Folkways;* Chapin, *Education and the Mores;* Keller, *Societal Evolution;* Veblen, *The Higher Learning in America;* Sinclair, *The Goose-Step;* Robinson, *The New History,* Chap. VIII; and *Mind in the Making.* Cf. also Dewey, *Democracy and Education;* and *The Schools of Tomorrow;* Stearns, *Civilization in the United States,* pp. 77–150; Lewisohn, *Up-Stream,* Chaps. VII–VIII.

CHAPTER XIII

POLITICAL THEORY AND THE SOCIAL ENVIRONMENT
OF THE WRITER

1. *Influence of the Social Environment upon the Doctrines of Representative Sociologists*

As soon as modern psychology had destroyed the notion that political theories were the product either of divine revelation or of innate ideas of the writers, it was easy to understand that some intimate relation existed between the political theories of a writer and the social and intellectual conditions in which he lived. This reflection of environment in a writer's political theories has been in some cases a faithful rendition of the majority opinion and in others a vigorous reaction against it, with, of course, all possible variations between these two extremes. Illustrations of this relation between social environment and political theory may be seen in the influence of the French Revolution upon Comte and his utilization of its lessons in the effort to remedy the evils of early French industrial society; in Spencer's reflection of the political and economic individualism of England in the middle of the nineteenth century and the development of evolutionary biology in the generation following; in Tarde's experience with social repetition as a judge and his observation of imitation, repetition and the rapid contagion of ideas in French society; in Durkheim's realization of the psychic unity of French social groups and their domination over the individual, and his experience with Anti-Semitism; in Kropotkin's negative reaction to Russian autocracy and European capitalism and militarism; in the repulsion of Novicow by similar conditions; in the emphasis laid by Gumplowicz and Ratzenhofer on the importance of the struggle of ethnic and social groups, a process that they had ample opportunity for investigating and observing in their native Austria; in De Greef's concern with contractualism and international agreements which furnished the only guarantee of the political integrity of his own country, Belgium; in the influence of a positive theory of the state and neo-socialistic doctrines on Hobhouse and Wallas, as a result of the dominating progressive tendencies in England from 1885 onward; in the influence upon Ross of the abuses of plutocratic society in contemporary America, and of the progressive and liberal spirit of Wisconsin; in Stein's reflection of authoritarian and constructive social reform doctrines in Germany and Switzerland; in the importance for Giddings' doctrines of the growth of American prosperity and power since 1870, as well as the problems of immigration and assimilation which have arisen since that time; in Veblen's reaction against plutocracy and the wastes of the practical operation of the "theory of business enterprise," which he observed from the special vantage point of Chicago, in the country where these excesses have been carried to the greatest extreme, and where economic factors have gained an unusual degree of ascendency over the other phases of life.

2. *Giddings' Synthetic Hypothesis of the Social Determination of Political Theory*

Many sociologists have called attention to this inevitable relation between social and political conditions and contemporary social and political theory, but the most daring and ambitious effort to present a synthetic interpretation of the problem has been made by Giddings. He has traced the manner in which the social and cultural conditions grow out of those circumstances in the natural geographical environment which determine the number and types of peoples who will dwell in any area and produce the material conditions of their life.[1] Next, he has attempted to classify the various possible types of society and to indicate the variety of social and political theory which will dominate in each. The essential phases of this contribution are contained in the following citation:[2]

First, there are types or kinds of societies. The broadest groupings correspond to the familiar demarkations made by Natural History. There are animal societies and human societies; and the human societies are further divided into the ethnic—or communities of kindred, and the civil—or communities composed of individuals that dwell and work together without regard to their blood relationships.

More significant for the sociologist, however, is a classification based on psychological characteristics. The fundamental division now is into instinctive and rational societies. The bands, swarms, flocks, and herds in which animals live and cooperate, are held together by instinctive

[1] "Theory of Social Causation," loc. cit.
[2] "Concepts and Methods of Sociology," in *American Journal of Sociology*, Vol. X, pp. 166 ff.

and not by rational comprehension of the utility of association. Their like-responses to stimulus, their imitative acts, the frequent appearance among them of impression and submission, are all purely instinctive phenomena. Not so are the social relations of human beings. There is no human community in which instinctive like-response to stimulation is not complicated by some degree of rational comprehension of the utility of association.

The combinations, however, of instinct and reason are of many gradations; and the particular combination found in any given community determines its modes of like-response to stimulus and its consciousness of kind—establishes for it a dominant mode of the relation of mind to mind, or, as Tarde would have phrased it, of the inter-mental activity. This dominant mode of inter-mental activity—inclusive of like-response and the consciousness of kind—is the chief social bond of the given community, and it affords the best distinguishing mark for a classification of any society on psychological grounds. So discriminated, the kinds of rational or human societies are eight, as follows:

1. There is a homogeneous community of blood-relatives, composed of individuals that from infancy have been exposed to a common environment and to like circumstances, and who, therefore, by heredity and experience are alike. Always conscious of themselves as kindred, their chief social bond is sympathy. The kind or type of society, therefore, that is represented by a group of kindred may be called the Sympathetic.

2. There is a community made up of like spirits, gathered perhaps from widely distant points, and perhaps originally strangers, but drawn together by their common response to a belief or dogma, or to an opportunity for pleasure or improvement. Such is the religious colony, like the "Mayflower" band, or the Latter-Day Saints; such is the partisan political colony, like the Missouri and the New England settlements in Kansas; and such is the communistic brotherhood, like Icaria. Similarity of nature and agreement in ideas constitute the social bond, and the kind of society

so created is therefore appropriately called the Congenial.

3. There is a community of miscellaneous and sometimes lawless elements, drawn together by economic opportunity—the frontier settlement, the cattle range, the mining camp. The newcomer enters this community an uninvited but unhindered probationer, and remains in it on sufferance. A general approbation of qualities and conduct is practically the only social bond. This type of society, therefore, I venture to call the Approbational.

The three types of society thus far named are simple, spontaneously formed groups. The first two are homogeneous, and are usually found in relatively isolated environments. The third is heterogeneous, and has a transitory existence where exceptional economic opportunities are discovered on the confines of established civilizations.

Societies of the remaining five types are in a measure artificial, in part created by reflection—by conscious planning. They are usually compound, products of conquest or of federation, and, with few if any exceptions, they are of heterogeneous composition. They are found in the relatively bountiful and differentiated environments.

4. A community of the fourth type consists of elements widely unequal in ability: the strong and the weak, the brave and the timorous, exploiters and the exploited—like enough conquerors and conquered. The social bonds of this community are despotic power and a fear-inspired obedience. The social type is Despotic.

5. In any community of the fifth type arbitrary power has been established long enough to have identified itself with tradition and religion. Accepted as divinely right, it has become authority. Reverence for authority is the social bond, and the social type is, therefore, the Authoritative.

6. Society of the sixth type arises in populations that, like the Italian cities at their worst estate, have suffered disintegration of a pre-existing social order. Unscrupulous adventurers come forward and create relations of personal allegiance by means of bribery, patronage, and preferment.

Intrigue and conspiracy are the social bonds. The social type is the Conspirital.

7. Society of the seventh type is deliberately created by agreement. The utility of association has been perceived, and a compact of cooperation is entered into for the promotion of the general welfare. Such was the Achæan League. Such was the League of the Iroquois. Such was the confederation of American Commonwealths in 1778. The social bond is a covenant or contract. The social type is the Contractual.

8. Society of the eighth type exists where a population collectively responds to certain great ideals, that, by united efforts, it strives to realize. Comprehension of mind by mind, confidence, fidelity, and an altruistic spirit of social service, are the social bonds. The social type is the Idealistic.

Of these varieties of society the higher, compound communities, or commonwealths, may, and usually do, include examples of the lower types, among their component groups.

All of these eight types, and the instinctive type exhibited by animal bands, have been observed from the earliest times and have suggested to social philosophers as many different theories of the nature of society. Thus in the totemistic lore of savagery we find endless suggestions of an instinct theory. In the mythologies of tribally organized barbarians we find sympathy, or natural-brotherhood theories, which later on are borrowed, adapted, and generalized by the great humanitarian religions, like Buddhism and Christianity. Suggested by societies of congenial spirits we have the consciousness-of-kind theories, voiced in the proverb that "birds of a feather flock together," in the saying of Empedocles that "like desires like," in the word of Ecclesiasticus that "all flesh consorteth according to kind, and a man will cleave to his like." From approbational societies have come our natural-justice theories. From despotic societies have come our political-sovereignty theories that "might makes right," in the sense of creating law and order. From au-

thoritative societies have come theories of the divine right
of kings; from conspirital societies have come Machiavellian
theories of the inevitableness of intrigue and conspiracy; and
from societies long used to deliberative assemblies, to char-
ters of liberty and bills of rights, have come the social-
covenant or contract theories of Hobbes, Locke, and Rousseau. Finally, from societies that have attained the heights
of civilization have come the Utopian theories, from Plato
until now.

3. *Complexes of Individual Writers and their Social Theory*

Perhaps the most significant addition to our knowledge
of the basis of differences in social and political theory on
the part of writers born and reared in much the same social
environment has come from analytical and dynamic psychology. This subject has made it clear that the reactions of an individual to his environment are conditioned
to a large degree by the mental complexes which he has
built up as the result of his individual experiences. These
conditioned reactions to general social and political problems give color to the social and political theory of all
writers. There can be no doubt that social and economic
interests play their part in individual reactions and ration-
alizations, but the type of reaction is fundamentally determined by the complexes of the individual writer. One
cannot, for example, conceive of Alexander Hamilton as
the leader of a party with a negative policy toward the
state, even though he had been born a Virginia landlord,
nor of Thomas Jefferson as a constructive statesman if
he had been reared in association with the business interests of New York City during the period of the Revo-

lution and the Confederation. No one doubts that the personal experiences and complexes of men like Herbert Spencer had an overwhelming importance in the development of their social and political thinking.

While this notion of the basis of political and social theory involves the consideration of the influence of the political and social environment, it approaches the analysis of the environmental influences in a much more discriminating and differential manner than does Giddings in his theory of social causation. In addition to the general social conditions in which a theorist may live, there must be considered all the intimate facts of his personal experience which may in any way have affected his mental complexes and orientation. Yet this approach to the analysis of political theory need in no way be regarded as a negation of Giddings' theory. Rather it is an indispensable supplement to the more generalized theory of group determination of social and political doctrine.[3]

[3] Barnes, "Psychology and History," in *American Journal of Psychology*, Oct. 1919; "The Service of Analytical Psychology to History," in *Psychoanalytic Review*, Jan. 1921; Blanchard, "A Psychoanalytical Study of Auguste Comte," in *American Journal of Psychology*, April, 1918; Smith, "Luther's Early Development in the Light of Psychoanalysis," in *American Journal of Psychology*, July, 1913; Kallen, in *Harvard Theological Review*, July, 1920, pp. 306-10; O'Higgins, "The American Mind," in *McClure's Magazine*, Vol. 53; Jung, *Psychological Types;* Ogburn, "Bias, Psycho-analysis, and the Subjective in relation to Social Science," in *Publications of the American Sociological Society*, Vol. XVII, pp. 62-74; Rivers, *Psychology and Politics.*

SOME IMPORTANT BOOKS ON
SOCIOLOGY AND POLITICAL THEORY

ADAMS, BROOKS (1848–   )

The Theory of Social Revolutions. New York, Macmillan, 1913, 240 pp.

ALENGRY, FRANCK (1865–   )

Essai historique et critique sur la sociologie chez Auguste Comte. Paris, Alcan, 1900, 512 pp.

ALTHUSIUS, JOHANNES (1557–1638)

Politica methodice digesta atque exemplis et profanis illustrata; cui in fine adjuncta est oratio panegyrica, de necessitate, utilitate et antiquitate scholarum. Herbornae, Typis Corvinianis, 1625, 1003 pp.

AMMON, OTTO (1842–   )

Die Gesellschaftsordnung und ihre natürlichen Grundlagen: Entwurf einer Sozialanthropologie zum Gebrauch für all Gebildeten, die sich mit sozialen Fragen befassen. Jena, Fischer, 1895, 408 pp.

BAGEHOT, WALTER (1826–1877)

Physics and Politics; or thoughts on the application of the principles of "natural selection" and "inheritance" to political society. New York, Appleton, 1877, 228 pp.

BAILEY, WILLIAM BACON (1873–   )

Modern Social Conditions: a statistical study of birth, marriage, divorce, death, disease, suicide, immigration, etc., with special reference to the United States. New York, Century Co., 1906, 377 pp.

BALDWIN, JAMES MARK (1861–   )

The Individual and Society; or Psychology and Sociology. Boston, Badger, 1911, 210 pp.

Mental Development in the Child and the Race: methods and processes. New York, Macmillan, 1895, 477 pp. (3rd rev. ed. 1906.)

Social and Ethical Interpretations in Mental Development: a study in social psychology. New York, Macmillan, 1897, 574 pp. (4th ed. 1906.)

BARKER, ERNEST (1874–   )

Political Thought in England from Spencer to the Present Day. New York, Holt, 1915, 256 pp. (Home University.)

BARTH, PAUL (1858–   )

Die Philosophie der Geschichte als Sociologie. Leipzig Reisland, 1897, Part I, 396 pp. (4th rev. and enl. ed., 1922, Vol. I.)

BATESON, WILLIAM (1861–   )

Biological Fact and the Structure of Society. (The Herbert Spencer Lecture delivered at the examination schools in February, 1912.) Oxford, Clarendon Press, 1916, 34 pp.

BEARD, CHARLES AUSTIN (1874–   )

Contemporary American History. New York, Macmillan, 1914, 397 pp.

The Economic Basis of Politics. New York, Knopf, 1922, 99 pp.

BELLOC, HILAIRE (1870–   )

The Servile State. London, Foulis, 1912, 188 pp.

BENOIST, CHARLES (1861–   )

La crise de l'état moderne. Paris, Firmin-Didot, 1897, 453 pp.

BENTLEY, ARTHUR FISHER (1870–   )

The Process of Government: a study of social pressures. Chicago, University of Chicago Press, 1908, 501 pp.

BOAS, FRANZ (1858–   )

The Mind of Primitive Man. New York, Macmillan, 1911, 294 pp.

BOGARDUS, EMORY STEPHEN (1882–)

Essentials of Social Psychology. Los Angeles, University of Southern California Press, 1920, 304 pp.

A History of Social Thought. Los Angeles, University of Southern California Press, 1922, 510 pp.

BOWLEY, ARTHUR LYON (1869–)

The Division of the Product of Industry. Oxford, Clarendon Press, 1919, 60 pp.

Wages in the United Kingdom in the Nineteenth Century. Cambridge, England, University Press, 1900, 148 pp.

BRAILSFORD, HENRY NOEL (1873–)

Shelly, Godwin, and their Circle. New York, Holt, 1913, 256 pp. (Home University Library.)

BRISTOL, LUCIUS MOODY

Social Adaptation. Cambridge, Massachusetts, Harvard University Press, 1915, 356 pp. (Preface by Thomas Nixon Carver.)

BROOKS, ROBERT CLARKSON (1874–)

Corruption in American Politics and Life. New York, Dodd-Mead, 1910, 309 pp.

BROWN, WILLIAM JETHRO (1868–)

The Underlying Principles of Modern Legislation. London, Murray, 1914, 319 pp. (6th ed. 1920).

BRUN, CHARLES (1870–)

Le régionalisme. Paris, Bloud, 1911, 289 pp.

BRUNHES, JEAN (1869–)

Human Geography: an attempt at a positive classification, principles and methods. Chicago, Rand-McNally, 1920, 648 pp. (Translated from the French by T. C. LeCompte, edited by Isaiah Bowman.)

BRUNHES, JEAN (1869–)

VALLAUX, CAMILLE (1870–)

La géographie de l'histoire; géographie de la paix et de
la guerre sur terre et sur mer.   Paris, Alcan, 1921, 715 pp.
BRYCE, JAMES BRYCE, Viscount, (1838–1922)

The American Commonwealth.   New and London, Macmillan, 1893, 2 vols. (rev. ed. 1909.)

Modern Democracies, New York, Macmillan, 1921, 2 vols.
BUELL, RAYMOND LESLIE

Contemporary French Politics.   New York and London,
Appleton, 1920, 523 pp.   (Introduction by C. J. H. Hayes.)
BURGESS, JOHN WILLIAM (1844–   )

Political Science and Comparative Constitutional Law.
Boston and London, Ginn, 1890, 2 vols.
BURR, CLINTON STODDARD

America's Race Heritage.

New York, The National Historical Society, 1922, 337 pp.
BURY, JOHN BAGNELL (1861–   )

The Ancient Greek Historians.   New York, Macmillan,
1909, 281 pp.

The Idea of Progress: an inquiry into its origin and
growth.   London, Macmillan, 1920, 377 pp.
CARPENTER, NILES

Guild Socialism: an historical and critical analysis.   New
York and London, Appleton, 1922, 350 pp.
CARR-SAUNDERS, ALEXANDER MORRIS (1886–   )

The Problem of Population: a study in human evolution.
Oxford, Clarendon Press, 1922, 516 pp.
CARVER, THOMAS NIXON (1865–   )

Essays in Social Justice.   Cambridge, Massachusetts,
Harvard University Press, 1915, 429 pp.
CHAMBERLAIN, HOUSTON STEWART (1855–   )

The Foundations of the Nineteenth Century.   New York
and London, John Lane, 1911, 2 vols.   (Translated from
the German—Die Grundlagen des neunzehnten Jahrhun-
derts, Munich, Bruckmann, 1903, by John Lees, with an
Introduction by Lord Redesdale.)

CHAPIN, FRANCIS STUART (1888–   )
Education and the Mores: a sociological essay. New York, Longmans, 1911, 107 pp.

COKER, FRANCIS WILLIAM (1878–   )
Organismic Theories of the State: nineteenth century interpretations of the state as organism or as person. New York, Longmans, 1910, 209 pp.
Readings in Political Philosophy. New York, Macmillan, 1914, 573 pp.
Recent and Contemporary Political Theory. New York, Century, 1924.

COLE, GEORGE DOUGLAS HOWARD (1889–   )
Guild Socialism: a plan for economic democracy. New York, Stokes, 1921, 202 pp.
Social Theory. New York, Stokes; London, Methuen, 1920, 220 pp.

COMMONS, JOHN ROGERS (1862–   )
Races and Immigrants in America. New York and London, Macmillan, 1907, 242 pp.

COMTE, ISIDORE AUGUSTE MARIE FRANCOIS XAVIER (1798-1857)
System of a Positive Polity. London, Longmans, 1857–1877, 4 vols.

CONKLIN, EDWIN GRANT (1863–   )
The Direction of Human Evolution. New York, Scribner's, 1921, 247 pp.

COOLEY, CHARLES HORTON (1864–   )
Human Nature and the Social Order. New York, Scribner's, 1902, 413 pp.
Social Organization: a study of the larger mind. New York, Scribner's, 1909, 426 pp. (Rev. ed. 1920.)
Social Process. New York, Scribner's, 1918, 430 pp.

CORBIN, JOHN (1870–   )
The Return of the Middle Class. New York, Scribner's, 1922, 353 pp.

COWAN, ANDREW REID

Master-clues in World History. New York and London, Longmans, 1914, 331 pp.

COX, HAROLD (1859–)

The Problem of Population. London, Cape, 1923, 198 pp.

DAVENPORT, CHARLES BENEDICT (1866–)

Heredity in its Relation to Eugenics. New York, Holt, 1911, 287 pp.

DAVENPORT, FREDERICK MORGAN (1866–)

Primitive Traits in Religious Revivals: a study in mental and social evolution. New York, Macmillan, 1905, 323 pp.

DAVIS, MICHAEL MARKS (1879–)

Psychological Interpretations of Society. New York, Longmans, 1909, 260 pp.

DAY, JAMES ROSCOE (1845–1923)

My Neighbor the Workingman. New York, Abingdon Press, 1920, 373 pp.

The Raid on Prosperity, New York, Appleton, 1907, 351 pp.

DEALEY, JAMES QUAYLE (1861–)

Sociology: Its Development and Applications. New York, Appleton, 1920, 547 pp.

DEFOURNY, MAURICE (1878–)

La sociologie positiviste. Paris, Alcan, 1902, 370 pp.

DE GREEF, GUILLAUME JOSEPH (1842–)

La constituante et la régime representatif. Brussels, 1892, 338 pp.

L'évolution des croyances et des doctrines politiques. Brussels, Mayolez, 1895, 330 pp.

Introduction à la sociologie. Brussels, Mayolez, 1886–1889, 2 vols. (Paris, Riviere, 1911, 2 vols.)

La structure générale des sociétés. Brussels, Larcier, 1907–1908, 3 vols. in 2. (Translated in large part in the American Journal of Sociology, Vols. VIII-X, 1902–4.)

Le transformisme social. Paris, Alcan, 1895, 520 pp.

DEMOLINS, EDMOND (1852–1907)

Anglo-Saxon Superiority: to What is it Due? London, The Leadenhall Press, 1899, 427 pp. (Translated from the French by Louis B. Lavigne.)

Comment la route crée la type sociale. Paris, Firmin-Didot, no date, 2 vols. (English translation announced.)

DETMOLD, CHRISTIAN EDWARD (1810–87)

The Historical Political and Diplomatic Writings of Nicolo Machiaveli. Boston, Osgood, 1882, 4 vols.

DEVINE, EDWARD THOMAS (1867–   )

Efficiency and Relief: a program of social work. New York, Columbia University, 1906, 45 pp.

DEWEY, JOHN (1859–   )

Democracy and Education. New York, Macmillan, 1916, 434 pp.

Human Nature and Conduct: an introduction to social psychology. New York, Holt, 1922, 336 pp.

The Schools of Tomorrow. New York, Dutton, 1915, 316 pp.

DEXTER, EDWIN GRANT (1868–   )

Weather Influences: an empirical study of the mental and physiological effects of definite meteorological conditions. New York, Macmillan, 1904, 286 pp. (With an Introduction by C. Abbe.)

DICKINSON, ZENAS CLARK

Economic Motives: a study in the psychological foundations of economic theory. Cambridge, Massachusetts, Harvard University Press, 1922, 304 pp.

DUGUIT, LÉON (1859–   )

Law in the Modern State. New York, Huebsch, 1919, 247 pp. (Translated from the French by Frida and Harold Laski.)

Traité du droit constitutionnel. Paris, Fontemoing, 1911, 2 vols. (New ed. 1921–   )

DUMONT, ARSÈNE (1849–1902)

Dépopulation et civilisation: étude démographique. Paris,
Lecrosnier, 1890, 520 pp.

DUNNING, WILLIAM ARCHIBALD (1857–1922)

A History of Political Theories: ancient and medieval.
New York, Macmillan, 1902, 360 pp.

A History of Political Theories from Luther to Montesquieu. New York, Macmillan, 1905, 459 pp.

A History of Political Theories from Rousseau to Spencer.
New York, Macmillan, 1920, 446 pp.

DUPRAT, GUILLAUME (1872–   )

La solidarité sociale: ses causes, son évolution, ses con-
séquences. Paris, Doin, 1907, 354 pp. (Preface by M. G.
Richard.)

Morals: a treatise on the psycho-sociological bases of
ethics. London, Scott, 1903, 382 pp. (Translated by
W. J. Greenstreet.)

DURKHEIM, EMILÉ (1858–1917)

De la division du travail social. Paris, Alcan, 1893, 471
pp. (2nd ed. 1902, 3rd ed. 1911)

Les règles de la méthode sociologique. Paris, Alcan, 1895,
186 pp. (6th ed. 1912.)

Le suicide: étude de sociologie. Paris, Alcan, 1897,
462 pp.

EDDY, ARTHUR JEROME (1857–1920)

Property, Chicago, McClurg, 1921, 254 pp.

EDMAN, IRWIN (1896–   )

Human Traits and their Social Significance. Boston and
New York, Houghton Mifflin, 1920, 467 pp.

ELLWOOD, CHARLES ABRAM (1873–   )

The Social Problem. New York, Macmillan, 1915, 255 pp.

Sociology in its Psychological Aspects. New York,
Appleton, 1912, 416 pp. (2nd ed. 1921.)

Sociology and Modern Social Problems. New York and
Cincinnati, American Book Company, 1919, 416 pp.

EXLINE, FRANK

Politics. New York, Dutton, 1922, 226 pp.

FAGUET, ÉMILE (1847–1916)

The Cult of Incompetence. London, Murray; New York, Dutton, 1911, 236 pp. (Translated from the French by Beatrice Barstow, with an Introduction by Thomas Mackay.)

FAIRCHILD, HENRY PRATT (1880–   )

Immigration: a world movement and its American significance. New York, Macmillan, 1913, 455 pp.

FIGGIS, JOHN NEVILLE (1866–   )

Churches in the Modern State. New York and London, Longmans, 1914 (2nd ed.), 272 pp.

FISKE, JOHN (1842–1901)

American Political Ideas, viewed from ᵗhe standpoint of universal history. New York and Boston, Houghton Mifflin, 1911, 196 pp.

FLINT, ROBERT (1838–1910)

History of the Philosophy of History in France, French Belgium, and Switzerland. New York, Scribner's 1894, 706 pp.

The Philosophy of History in Europe: France and Germany. London, Blackwood, 1874, 609 pp.

FOLLETT, MARY PARKER (1868–   )

The New State: group organization the solution of popular government. New York, Longmans, 1918, 373 pp. (Introduction by Lord Haldane.)

FORD, HENRY JONES (1851–   )

The Natural History of the State: an introduction to political science. Princeton, Princeton University Press, 1915, 188 pp.

Rise and Growth of American Politics: a sketch of constitutional development. New York and London, Macmillan, 1898, 409 pp.

FOUILLÉE, ALFRED JULES ÉMILE (1838–1912)
La science sociale contemporaine. Paris, Hachette, 1910, 424 pp.

FRANK, GLEN (1887–)
The Politics of Industry, a foot note to the social unrest. New York, Century, 1919, 214 pp.

FRAZER, SIR JAMES GEORGE (1854–)
Totemism and Exogamy: a treatise on certain early forms of superstition and society. London, Macmillan, 1910, 4 vols.

FREUND, ERNST (1864–)
Standards of American Legislation: an estimate of restrictive and constructive factors. Chicago, Chicago University Press, 1917, 327 pp.

GALTON, SIR FRANCIS (1822–1911)
Hereditary Genius. London, Macmillan, 1869, 390 pp. (new ed. 1892)
Inquires into Human Faculty and its Development. London, Dent; New York, Dutton, 1908, 261 pp.
Natural Inheritance. London, Macmillan, 1889, 259 pp.

GARNER, JAMES WILFORD (1871–)
Introduction to Political Science: a treatise on the origin, nature, functions, and organization of the state. New York, American Book Company, 1910, 616 pp.

GEDDES, PATRICK (1854–)
Cities in Evolution: an introduction to the town planning movement and to the study of civics. London, Williams & Norgate, 1915, 409 pp.

GEDDES, PATRICK (1854–)
BRANFORD, VICTOR
The Coming Polity: a study in reconstruction. London, Williams & Norgate, 1919, 332 pp.

GEHLKE, CHARLES E.
Emile Durkheim's Contributions to Sociological Theory. New York, Longmans, 1915, 188 pp.

GETTELL, RAYMOND GARFIELD (1881–   )

Problems in Political Evolution. Boston, Ginn, 1914, 400 pp.

GIDDINGS, FRANKLIN HENRY (1855–   )

Democracy and Empire: with studies of their psychological, economic and moral foundations. New York, Macmillan, 1900, 363 pp.

The Elements of Sociology: a text-book for colleges and schools. New York, Macmillan, 1898, 353 pp.

Inductive Sociology: a syllabus of methods, analyses and classifications and provisionally formulated laws. New York, Macmillan, 1901, 302 pp.

The Principles of Sociology: an analysis of the phenomena of association and of social organization. New York, Macmillan, 1896, 476 pp.

Readings in Descriptive and Historical Sociology, New York, Macmillan, 1906, 553 pp.

The Responsible State: a reexamination of fundamental political doctrines in the light of world war and the menace of anarchism. New York and Boston, Houghton, Mifflin, 1918, 107 pp.

Studies in Theory of Human society. New York, Macmillan, 1922, 308 pp.

GIERKE, OTTO FRIEDRICH von (1841–   )

Das deutsche Genossenschaftsrecht. Berlin, Weidmann, 1868–1881, 4 vols.

Die Genossenschaftstheorie und die deutsche Rechtsprechung. Berlin, Weidmann, 1887, 1024 pp.

Johannes Althusius und die Entwicklung der naturrechtlichen Staatstheorien. Breslau, Koebner, 1880, 322 pp.

GINI, CORRADO

Problemi sociologici della Guerra. Bologna, Zanichelli, 1921, 395 pp.

GOBINEAU, JOSEPH ARTHUR, Comte de (1816–1882)

Essay on the Inequality of the Human Races. New York,

Putnam's, 1915, 217 pp. (Translated from the French by Adrian Collins, with an Introduction by Oscar Levy.)

GODDARD, HENRY BUHERT (1866–   )

Human Efficiency and Levels of Intelligence. Princeton, Princeton University Press, 1920, 128 pp.

GOLDENWEISER, ALEXANDER A.

Early Civilization; an introduction to anthropology. New York, Knopf, 1922, 424 pp.

GOODNOW, FRANK JOHNSON (1859–   )

Politics and Administration: a study in government. New York and London, Macmillan, 1900, 270 pp.

Social Reform and the Constitution. New York, Macmillan, 1911, 365 pp.

GOULD, CHARLES W.

America: a family matter. New York, Scribner's, 1922, 193 pp.

GRANT, MADISON (1865–   )

The Passing of the Great Race, New York, Scribner's, 1918, 296 pp.

GRAY, BENJAMIN KIRKMAN (1862–1907)

Philanthropy and the State: or social politics. London, King, 1908, 339 pp.

GUMPLOWICZ, LUDWIG (1838–1909)

Grundriss der Sociologie. Vienna, Manz, 1885, 246 pp. (Translated—The Outlines of Sociology by F. W. Moore, Publications of the American Academy of Political and Social Science, Philadelphia, 1899, 229 pp.)

Rasse und Staat, Innsbruck, Wagner, 1875.

Der Rassenkampf: sociologische Untersuchungen. Innsbruck, Wagner, 1883, 376 pp. (French translation, La lutte des races.)

HALL, GRANVILLE STANLEY (1846–   )

Adolescence: its psychology and its relations to physiology, anthropology, sociology, sex, crime, religion, and education. New York, Appleton, 1905, 2 vols.

Morâle: the supreme standard of life and conduct. New York, Appleton, 1920, 377 pp.

HANKINS, FRANK HAMILTON (1877–   )
Adolphe Quetelet as Statistician. New York, Longmans, 1908, 135 pp.
The Racial Basis of Civilization. New York, Knopf, 1924.

HANSEN, GEORG
Die drei Bevölkerungsstufen: ein Versuch, die Ursachen für das Blühen und Altern der Volker nachzuweisen. Munich, Lindauer, 1889, 407 pp. (New ed. 1915.)

HAWORTH, PAUL LELAND (1876–   )
America in Ferment. Indianapolis, Bobbs-Merrill, 1915, 477 pp.

HAYES, EDWARD CARY (1868–   )
Introduction to the Study of Sociology. New York, Appleton, 1915, 715 pp.

HECKER, JULIUS FREDERICK
Russian Sociology. New York, Longmans, 1916, 309 pp.

HELMOLT, HANS FERDINAND (1865–   )
The World's History. London, Heinemann, 1901–7, 8 vols.

HOBBES, THOMAS (1588–1679)
Leviathan. London, Routledge, 1886, 320 pp. (Introduction by H. Morley)

HOBHOUSE, LEONARD TRELAWNEY (1864–   )
Democracy and Reaction. London, Unwin, 1904, 244 pp.
Development and Purpose: an essay towards a philosophy of evolution. London, Macmillan, 1913, 383 pp.
The Elements of Social Justice. London, Allen & Unwin, 1922, 208 pp.
Liberalism. New York, Holt, 1911, 254 pp. (Home University Library series.)
The Metaphysical Theory of the State: a criticism. London, Allen & Unwin; New York, Macmillan, 1918, 156 pp.
Morals in Evolution. London, Chapman & Hall; New York, Holt, 1906, 2 vols. (New ed. 1915)

230 Sociology and Political Theory

Questions of War and Peace. London, Unwin, 1916, 223 pp.

Social Evolution and Political Theory. New York, Columbia University, 1911, 218 pp.

The World in Conflict. London, Unwin, 1915, 104 pp.

HOBSON, JOHN ATKINSON (1858–   )

Evolution of Modern Capitalism: a study of machine production. London, Scott, 1910, 450 pp.

Imperialism. London, Nisbet, 1902, 400 pp.

The Social Problem: life and work. London, Allen & Unwin, 1922, 208 pp.

Work and Wealth: a human valuation. New York, Macmillan, 1914, 367 pp.

HOLCOMBE, ARTHUR NORMAN (1884–   )

The Foundations of the Modern Commonwealth. New York, Harpers, 1923, 491 pp.

HOLMES, SAMUEL JACKSON (1868–   )

The Trend of the Race: a study of present tendencies in the biological development of civilized mankind. New York, Harcourt-Brace, 1921, 396 pp.

HOWARD, GEORGE ELLIOTT (1849–   )

History of Matrimonial Institutions. Chicago, Chicago University Press, 1904, 3 vols.

HULBERT, ARCHER BUTLER (1873–   )

Historic Highways of America. Cleveland, A. H. Clark Co., 1902, 1905, 16 vols.

HUME, DAVID (1711–1776)

Essays, Literary, Moral, and Political. London, Longmans, 1875, 2 vols.

HUNTINGTON, ELLSWORTH (1876–   )

Civilization and Climate. New Haven, Yale University Press, 1915, 333 pp.

Climatic Changes, their Nature and Causes. New Haven, Yale University Press, 1922, 329 pp.

The Pulse of Asia: a journey in Central Asia illustrating the geographic basis of history. Boston, Houghton, Mifflin, 1907, 415 pp.

World-Power and Evolution. New Haven, Yale University Press, 1919, 287 pp.

HYNDMAN, HENRY MAYERS (1842–1921)

The Evolution of Revolution. London, Grant Richards; New York, Boni & Liveright, 1921, 406•pp.

JACOBS, PHILIP PETER (1879–   )

German Sociology. New York, privately printed, 1909, 105 pp.

JACOBY, PAUL

Études sur la sélection chez l'homme. Paris, Alcan, 1904, 620 pp. (Avantpropos par Gabriel Tarde.)

JAMES, WILLIAM (1842–1910)

The Principles of Psychology. New York, Holt, 1905, 2 vols.

The Will to Believe, and other Essays in Popular Philosophy. New York, Longmans, 1897, 332 pp.

JENKS, EDWARD (1861–   )

The State and the Nation. New York, Dutton, 1919, 312 pp.

JENKS, JEREMIAH WHIPPLE (1856–   )

LAUCK, W. JETT (1879–   )

The Immigration Problem: a study of American Immigration conditions and needs. New York, Funk & Wagnalls, 1913, 551 pp. (5th rev. ed. 1922.)

JENKS, JEREMIAH WHIPPLE (1856–   )

Governmental Action for Social Welfare. New York, Macmillan, 1910, 226 pp. (American Social Progress Series.)

JUNG, CARL GUSTAV (1875–   )

Psychological Types. New York, Harcourt Brace, 1923, 654 pp.

KALES, ALBERT MARTIN (1875–   )
Unpopular Government in the United States. Chicago, Chicago University Press, 1914, 263 pp.

KELLER, ALBERT GALLOWAY (1874–   )
Societal Evolution; a study of the evolutionary basis of the science of society. New York, Macmillan, 1915, 338 pp.

KELLICOTT, WILLIAM ERSPINE (1878–   )
The Social Direction of Human Evolution. New York, Appleton, 1911, 249 pp.

KIDD, BENJAMIN (1858–1916)
The Control of the Topics. New York, Macmillan, 1898, 101 pp.
Social Evolution. New York and London, Macmillan, 1894. 348 pp. (New York, Putnam, rev. ed., 1921, 404 pp.)

KOLLER, ARMIN HAJMAN
The Theory of Environment: Menasha, Wisconsin, Banta Publishing Co., 1918, 104 pp.

KOREN, JOHN, editor, (1861–   )
The History of Statistics: their development and progress in many countries. New York, Macmillan, 1918, 777 pp.

KRABBE, HUGO (1857–   )
The Modern Idea of the State. New York, Appleton, 1922, 281 pp. (Translated by Sabine & Shepard.)

KROEBER, ALFRED L. (1876–   )
Anthropology. New York, Harcourt-Brace, 1923.

KROPOTKIN, PIOTR ALEKSYEYEVICH, Prince (1842–1921)
Mutual Aid: a factor of evolution. London, Heinemann, 1904, 348 pp.

LASKI, HAROLD JOSEPH (1893–   )
Authority in the Modern State. New Haven, Yale University Press, 1919, 398 pp.
The Foundations of Sovereignty. New York, Harcourt-Brace, 1921, 317 pp.

The Problem of Administrative Areas: an essay in reconstruction. Northampton, Smith College, 1918, 64 pp.

Studies in the Problem of Sovereignty. New Haven, Yale University Press, 1917, 297 pp.

LE BON, GUSTAV (1841–   )

The Crowd: a study of the popular mind. London, Unwin, 1917, 239 pp.

The Psychology of Peoples. London, Unwin, 1899, 230 pp.

La Psychologie politique et la défense sociale. Paris, Flammarion, 1910, 379 pp.

The Psychology of Revolution. New York, Putnam's, 1913, 337 pp.

The Psychology of Socialism. London, Unwin, 1899, 415 pp.

LE PLAY, PIERRE GUILLAUME FRÉDÉRIC (1806–1882)

L'Organisation de la famille. Tours, Marne, 1884, 520 pp.

La réforme sociale en France: déduite de l'observation comparée des peuples Européens. Tours, Marne et fils., 1878, 3 vols. (5th ed.)

LEVASSEUR, PIERRE EMILE (1828–1911)

La population francaise: historie de la population avant 1879, et demographie de la France comparée à celle des autres nations au XIXe siècle precede d'une introduction sur la statistique. Paris, Rousseau, 1889–1892, 3 vols.

LEVINE, LOUIS (1883–   )

Syndicalism in France. New York, Longmans, 1914, 229 pp. (Introduction by Franklin H. Giddings.)

LICHTENBERGER, JAMES PENDLETON (1870–   )

The Development of Social Theory. New York, Century, 1923, 482 pp.

LILIENFELD, PAUL DE (1829–1903)

La pathologie sociale. Paris, Giard et Brière, 1896, 336 pp. (Avec une introduction de René Worms.)

Gedanken uber die Sozialwissenschaft der Zukunft. Mitau, 1873–1881, 5 vols.

LIPPMANN, WALTER (1889–   )

Drift and Mastery: an attempt to diagnose the current unrest. New York, Kennerly, 1914, 334 pp.

Liberty and the News. New York, Harcourt-Brace, 1920, 104 pp.

A Preface to Politics. New York, Kennerly, 1913, 318 pp.

Public Opinion. New York, Harcourt-Brace, 1922, 427 pp.

LOCKE, JOHN (1632–1704)

Two Treatises on Civil Government. London, Rutledge, 1884, 320 pp.

LORIA, ACHILLE (1857–   )

Aspetta sociali ed economici della guerra mondiale. Milan, Vallardi, 1921, 458 pp.

The Economic Foundations of Society. London, Sonnenschein: New York, Scribner's, 1899, 385 pp. (Translated from the 2nd French ed. by Lindley M. Keasby.)

LOWELL, ABBOTT LAWRENCE (1856–   )

Public Opinion and Popular Government. New York, Longmans, 1913, 415 pp.

Public Opinion in War and Peace, Cambridge, Massachusetts, Harvard University Press, 1922, 302 pp.

LOWENTHAL, ESTHER (1883–   )

The Ricardian Socialists. New York, Longmans, 1911, 107 pp.

LOWIE, ROBERT HARRY (1883–   )

Culture and Ethnology. New York, McMurtie, 1917, 189 pp.

Primitive Society. New York, Boni & Liveright, 1920, 463 pp.

MCBAIN, HOWARD LEE (1880–   )

ROGERS, LINDSAY (1891–   )

The New Constitutions of Europe. Garden City, Doubleday-Page, 1922, 612 pp.

MCDOUGALL, WILLIAM (1871–   )

An Introduction to Social Psychology. Boston, Luce, 1914, 431 pp.

The Group Mind: a sketch of the principles of social psychology, with some attempt to apply them to the interpretation of national life and character. New York, Putnams, 1920, 418 pp.

Is America Safe for Democracy? New York, Scribner's, 1921, 218 pp. (Lowell Lectures.)

MACIVER, ROBERT MORRISON (1882–   )

Community: a sociological study. London, Macmillan, 1917, 437 pp.

MACKINDER, HALFORD JOHN (1861–   )

Democratic Ideals and Reality: a study of the politics of reconstruction. London, Constable, 1919, 272 pp.

MAINE, HENRY SUMNER (1822–1888)

Ancient Law: its connection with the early history of society, and its relation to modern ideas. London, Murray, 1870, 415 pp.

MAITLAND, FREDERIC WILLIAM (1850–1906)

Introduction to Gierke's Political Theories of the Middle Age. Cambridge, England, University Press, 1900, 197 pp.

MALLOCK, WILLIAM HURRELL (1849–1923)

Aristocracy and Evolution: a study of the rights, the origin, and the social functions of the wealthier classes. London, Black, 1898, 385 pp.

A Critical Examination of Socialism. New York, Harper, 1907, 303 pp.

The Limits of the Pure Democracy. London, Chapman & Hall, 1918, 397 pp.

Social Reform as Related to Realities and Delusions. London, Murray, 1914, 391 pp.

MARETT, ROBERT RANULPH (1866–   )

Anthropology. London, Williams & Norgate, 1911, 256 pp. New York, Holt. (Home University Library.)

MARTINEAU, HARRIET (1802–1876)

The Positive Philosophy of August Comte (freely translated and condensed.)   London, Bell, 1896, 3 vols.

MAYO-SMITH, RICHMOND (1854–1901)

Statistics and Sociology.   New York, Macmillan, 1895, 399 pp.

MERRIAM, CHARLES EDWARD (1874–   )

American Political Ideas: studies in the development of American political thought.   New York, Macmillan, 1920, 481 pp.

History of American Political Theories.   New York and London, Macmillan, 1906, 364 pp.

MERZ, JOHN THEODORE (1840–   )

History of European Thought in the Nineteenth Century. Edinburgh, Blackwood, 1896, 4 vols.

METCHNIKOFF, LÉON (1838–1888)

La civilisation et les grandes fleuves historiques.   Paris, Hachette, 1889, 369 pp.   (With a Preface by Élisée Reclus.)

MICHELS, ROBERT (1876–   )

Political Parties: a sociological study of the oligarchical tendencies of modern democracy.   New York, Hearst's International Library Co., 1915, 416 pp.   (Translated from the French by Eden and Cedar Paul.)

MOON, PARKER THOMAS (1892–   )

The Labor Problem and the Catholic Social Movement in France.   New York, Macmillan, 1921, 473 pp.

MORLEY, JOHN (1838–1923)

Critical Miscellanies.   London, Macmillan, 1886–1913, 4 vols.

MUIR, JOHN RAMSAY BRYCE (1872–   )

Liberalism and Industry.   London, Constable, 1920, 208 pp.

Nationalism and Internationalism, the culmination of modern history.   London, Constable, 1917, 229 pp.

MYERS, GUSTAVUS (1872–   )

History of the Supreme Court of the United States. Chicago, Kerr, 1912, 823 pp.

History of the Great American Fortunes. Chicago, Kerr, 1911–17, 3 vols.

NEWSHOLME, SIR ARTHUR (1857–)

Elements of Vital Statistics. London, Sonnenschein, 1899, 326 pp.

NICOLAI, GEORG FRIEDRICH (1872–)

The Biology of War. New York, Century Co., 1918, 553 pp. (Translated from the German by Constance and Julian Grande.)

NITTI, FRANCESCO SAVERIO (1868–)

Catholic Socialism. London, Sonnenschein, 1895, 432 pp. (New ed. 1911.)

Population and the Social System. London, Sonnenschein, 1894, 192 pp.

NOVICOW, JACQUES (YAKOV ALEKSANDROVICH) (1849–1912)

L'affranchisement de la femme. Paris, Alcan, 1903, 267 pp.

Conscience et volonté sociales. Paris, Giard & Brière, 1897, 381 pp.

La critique du Darwinism social. Paris, Alcan, 1910, 406 pp.

La fédération de l'Europe. Paris, Alcan, 1901, 807 pp.

Les luttes entre sociétés humaines; et leurs phases successives. Paris, Alcan, 1893, 748 pp.

The Mechanism and Limits of Human Association. (Translated in the American Journal of Sociology, vol. XXIII, 1917, pp. 289–349.)

La politique internationale. Paris, Alcan, 1886, 393 pp.

War and its Alleged Benefits. New York, Holt, 1911, 130 pp. (Translated by Thomas Seltzer.)

OPPENHEIMER, FRANZ (1864–)

The State: its history and development viewed sociologically. Indianapolis, Bobbs-Merrill, 1914, 362 pp.

System der Soziologie. Jena, Fischer, 1923.

OGBURN, WILLIAM FIELDING (1886–   )
Social Change: with respect to culture and original nature. New York, Huebsch, 1922, 365 pp.

PARKER, CARLETON HUBBELL (1879–1918)
The Casual Laborer and Other Essays. New York, Harcourt-Brace 1920, 199 pp.

PARTRIDGE, GEORGE EVERETT (1870–   )
The Psychology of Nations: a contribution to the Philosophy of History. New York, Macmillan, 1919, 333 pp.

PATTEN, SIMON NELSON (1852–1922)
The New Basis of Civilization. New York, Macmillan, 1908, 220 pp.
Theory of Social Forces. Philadelphia, American Academy of Political and Social Sciences, 1895, 151 pp.

PAUL-BONCOUR, JOSEPH (1873–   )
La fédéralisme economique: etude sur les rapports de l'individu et des groupements professionnels. Paris, Alcan, 1900, 395 pp. (Preface de M. Waldeck-Rousseau.)

PEARSON, KARL (1857–   )
National Life from the Standpoint of Science. London, Black, 1905, 106 pp. (2nd ed.)

PILLSBURY, WALTER BOWERS (1872–   )
The Psychology of Nationality and Internationalism. New York, Appleton, 1919, 314 pp.

POSADA, ADOLFO (1860–   )
Théories modernes sur les origines de la famille, de la société et de l'état. Paris, Giard & Brière, 1896, 150 pp.

POUND, ROSCOE (1870–   )
An Introduction to the Philosophy of Law. New Haven, Yale University Press, 1922, 307 pp.
Interpretations of Legal History. New York, Macmillan, 1923, 171 pp.
The Spirit of the Common Law. Boston, Marshall-Jones, 1921, 224 pp.

RATZEL, FRIEDRICH (1844–1904)

Anthropogeographie. Stuttgart, Engelhorn, 1909–1912, 2 vols. (3rd ed.)

Politische Geographie. Munich, Oldenbourg, 1903, 838 pp. (2nd ed.)

Der Staat und sein Boden. Leipzig, Hirzel, 1897, 127 pp.

RATZENHOFER, GUSTAV (1842–1904)

Wesen und Zweck der Politik. Leipzig, Brockhaus, 1893, 3 vols.

Die sociologische Erkenntniss: positive Philosophie des socialen Lebens. Leipzig, Brockhaus, 1898, 372 pp.

Sociologie: positive Lehre von den menschlichen Wechselbeziehungen. Leipzig, Brockhaus, 1907, 231 pp.

RIPLEY, WILLIAM ZEBINA (1867–   )

The Races of Europe: a sociological study. New York, Appleton, 1899, 624 pp.

RITCHIE, DAVID GEORGE (1853–1903)

Natural Rights. London, Macmillan, 1895.

RIVERS, WILLIAM HALSE RIVERS (1864–1922)

Psychology and Politics. New York, Harcourt-Brace, 1923, 180 pp.

ROBINSON, JAMES HARVEY (1863–   )

The Humanizing of Knowledge. New York, Doran, 1923.

The New History: essays illustrating the modern historical outlook. New York, Macmillan, 1912, 266 pp.

The Mind in the Making. New York, Harpers, 1921, 235 pp.

ROSS, EDWARD ALSWORTH (1866–   )

Changing America: studies in contemporary society. New York, Century Co., 1912, 236 pp.

Foundations of Sociology. New York, Macmillan, 1905, 410 pp.

The Old World in the New: the significance of past and present immigration to the American people. New York, Century, 1914 327 pp.

The Principles of Sociology. New York, Century Co., 1920, 708 pp.

The Russian Bolshevik Revolution. New York, Century Co., 1921, 302 pp.

Russia in Upheaval. New York, Century Co., 1918, 354 pp.

Sin and Society: an analysis of latter-day iniquity. Boston, Houghton, Mifflin, 1907, 167 pp.

Social Control: a survey of the foundations of order. New York, Macmillan, 1904, 463 pp.

Social Psychology: an outline and source-book. New York, Macmillan, 1909, 372 pp.

The Social Trend. New York, Century Co. 1922, 235 pp.

SCHALLMAYER, WILHELM (1857–   )

Vererbung und Auslese im Lebenslauf der Völker: eine staatswissenschaftliche Studie auf Grund der neueren Biologie. Jena, Fischer, 1903, 386 pp.

SCHLESINGER, ARTHUR MEIER (1888–   )

New Viewpoints in American History. New York, Macmillan, 1922, 299 pp.

SEAGER, HENRY ROGERS (1870–   )

Social Insurance: a program of social reform. New York, Macmillan, 1910, 175 pp.

SELIGMAN, EDWIN ROBERT ANDERSON (1861–   )

The Economic Interpretation of History. New York, Columbia University Press, 1917, 166 pp.

SEMPLE, ELLEN CHURCHILL (1863–   )

Influences of Geographical Environment on the basis of Ratzel's system of anthropogeography. New York, Holt, 1911, 683 pp.

SERGI, GIUSEPPE (1841–   )

The Mediterranean Race: a study of the origin of European peoples. London, Scott; New York, Scribner's, 1901, 320 pp.

SHAND, ALEXANDER FAULKNER

The Foundations of Character: being a study of the tendencies of the emotions and sentiments. London, Macmillan, 1914, 532 pp.

SIDIS, BORIS (1867–1923)

The Psychology of Suggestion: a research into the subconscious nature of man and society. New York, Appleton, 1898, 386 pp. (With an Introduction by William James.)

SIGHELE, SCIPIO (1868–1913)

Contro il parlamentarismo. Saggio di psicologia collettiva. Milan, Treves, 1905.

La foule criminelle: essai de psychologie collective. Paris, Alcan, 1901, 300 pp.

Psychologie des sectes. Paris, Giard & Brière, 1898, 231 pp. (French translation by L. Brandin.)

SIMMEL, GEORG (1858–1918)

Soziologie: Untersuchungen uber die Formen der Vergesellschaftung. Leipzig, Dunker & Humblot, 1908, 782 pp. (Translated in large part in the American Journal of Sociology.)

SMALL, ALBION WOODBURY (1854–   )

Between Eras: from Capitalism to Democracy. Kansas City, Inter-Collegiate Press, 1913, 431 pp.

General Sociology. Chicago, Chicago University Press, 1905, 739 pp.

The Meaning of Social Science. Chicago, Chicago University Press, 1910, 309 pp.

SOMBART, WERNER (1863–   )

Der moderne Kapitalismus. Leipzig, Duncker & Humblot, 1902, 2 vols. (New ed. 1921)

The Quintessence of Capitalism: a study of the history and psychology of the modern business man. New York, Dutton, 1915, 400 pp. (Translated and edited by M. Epstein.)

SPENCER, HERBERT (1820–1903)

An Autobiography. New York, Appleton, 1904, 2 vols.

Essays, Scientific, Political, and Speculative. New York, Appleton, 1864, 362 pp.

Man versus the State. New York, Appleton, 1884, 113 pp.

The Principles of Sociology. New York, Appleton, 1877–1897, 3 vols.

The Study of Sociology. New York, Appleton, 1903, 411 pp.

SPENGLER, OSWALD (1880-)

Der Untergang des Abendlandes: eine Umriss einer Morphologie der Weltgeschichte. Munich, C. H. Breck, 1920, 2 vols.

SQUILLACE, FAUSTO

Die soziologische Theorien Liepzig, Klinkhardt, 1911, 352 pp.

STEIN, LUDWIG (1859-)

Einführung in die Soziologie. Munich, Rosel, 1921, 453 pp.

Philosophische Strömungen der Gegenwart. Stuttgart, Enke, 1908, 452 pp.

Die soziale Frage im Lichte der Philosophie: Vorlesungen uber Socialphilosophie und ihre Geschichte. Stuttgart, Enke, 1897, 791 pp. (new ed., 1923).

Der soziale Optimismus. Jena, Costenoble, 1905, 267 pp.

STUCKENBERG, JOHN HENRY WILBURN (1835-1903)

An introduction to the Study of Sociology. New York, Armstrong, 1898, 336 pp.

Sociology: the science of human society. New York, Putman, 1903, 2 vols.

SUMNER, WILLIAM GRAHAM (1840–1910)

The Challenge of Facts and Other Essays. New Haven, Yale University Press, 1913, 377 pp. (Edited by A. G. Keller).

Collected Essays in Political and Social Science. New York, Holt, 1885, 173 pp.

Earth Hunger and Other Essays. New Haven, Yale University Press, 1913, 377 pp. (Edited by A. G. Keller).

Folkways: a study of the sociological importance of usages, manners, customs, mores, and morals. Boston Ginn, 1907, 692 pp.

The Forgotten Man and Other Essays. New Haven, Yale University Press, 1918, 559 pp. (Edited by A. G. Keller).

War and Other Essays. New Haven, Yale University Press, 1911, 381 pp. (Edited by A. G. Keller).

What Social Classes Owe to Each Other. New York, Harpers, 1883, 169 pp.

SUTHERLAND, ALEXANDER (1852-1902)

The Origin and Growth of the Moral Instinct. London, Longmans, 1898, 2 vols.

SYBEL, HEINRICH VON (1817-1895)

History of the French Revolution. London, Murray, 1867–1869, 4 vols. (Translated from the 3rd German edition by W. C. Perry).

TARDE, GABRIEL DE (1843-1904)

The Laws of Imitation. New York, Holt, 1903, 404 pp. (Translated by Elsie Clews Parsons)

La logique sociale. Paris, Alcan, 1895, 464 pp.

L'opinion et la foule. Paris, Alcan, 1901, 226 pp.

Social Laws: an outline of sociology. New York, Macmillan, 1907, 213 pp. (Translated from the French by Howard C. Warren, with an Introduction by J. M. Baldwin).

Les transformations du pouvoir. Paris, Alcan, 1899. 266 pp.

TAWNEY, RICHARD HENRY (1880-)

The Acquisitive Society. New York, Harcourt-Brace, 1920, 188 pp.

TEAD, ORDWAY (1891-)

Instincts in Industry: a study in working-class psychology. Boston, Houghton Mifflin, 1918, 221 pp.

TEGGART, FREDERICK JOHN (1870-   )
The Processes of History. New Haven, Yale University Press, 1918, 162 pp.

TENNEY, ALVAN ALONZO (1876-   )
Social Democracy and Population. New York, Longmans, 1907, 89 pp.

THOMAS, WILLIAM ISAAC (1863-   )
The Polish Peasant in Europe and America. Boston, Badger, 1818–20, 5 vols.
Source Book for Social Origins. Chicago, University of Chicago Press, 1909, 932 pp.

THORNDIKE, EDWARD LEE (1874-   )
The Original Nature of Man. New York, Columbia University, 1913, 327 pp.

TODD, ARTHUR JAMES (1878-   )
Theories of Social Progress: a critical study of the attempts to formulate the conditions of human advance. New York, Macmillan, 1918, 579 pp.

TÖNNIES, FERDINAND (1885–   )
Kritik der öffentlichen Meinung. Berlin, Springer, 1922.
Gemeinschaft und Gesellschaft: Grundbegriffe der reinen Soziologie. Berlin, Curtius, 1920, 215 pp.

TREITSCHKE, HEINRICH GOTTHARD VON (1834–1896)
Politics. London, Constable, 1916, 2 vols. (Translated by Blanche Dugdale and Torben de Bille, with an Introduction by Arthur James Balfour).

TROTTER, W.
Instincts of the Herd in Peace and War. London, Unwin, 1916, 213 pp. (new ed. 1919).

VACCARO, MICHELE ANGELO (1854–   )
Les bases sociologiques du droit et de l'état. Paris, Giard & Brière, 1898, 480 pp.

VACHER DE LAPOUGE, GEORGES (1854–   )

Les séléctions sociales. Paris, Fontemoing, 1896, 503 pp.

VEBLEN, THORSTEIN B.

Absentee Ownership and Business Enterprise in Recent Times. The Case of America. New York, Huebsch, 1923.

The Engineers and the Price System. New York, Huebsch, 1921, 169 pp.

The Higher Learning in America: a memorandum on the conduct of universities by business men. New York, Huebsch, 1918, 286 pp.

The Nature of Peace and the Terms of its Perpetuation. New York, Macmillan, 1917, 367 pp.

Theory of Business Enterprise. New York Scribner's, 1904, 400 pp.

Theory of the Leisure Class: an economic study of the evolution of institutions. New York, Macmillan, 1899; Huebsch, 1918, 400 pp.

The Vested Interests and the State of the Industrial Arts. New York, Huebsch, 1919, 183 pp.

WALKER, GUY MORRISON (1870–   )

The Things that are Caesar's; a reference of wealth, New York, Fowle, 1922, 155 pp.

WALLAS, GRAHAM (1858–   )

The Great Society. New York, Macmillan, 1904, 383 pp.

Human Nature in Politics. Boston, Houghton Mifflin, 1908, 302 pp. (new ed. Knopf 1922)

Our Social Heritage. New Haven, Yale University Press, 1921, 307 pp.

WARD, LESTER FRANK (1841-1913)

Applied Sociology: a treatise on the conscious improvement of society by society. New York, Ginn, 1906, 384 pp.

Dynamic Sociology: or applied social science as based upon statistical sociology and the less complex sciences. New York, Appleton, 1883, 2 vols. (new ed., 1910)

Glimpses of the Cosmos: a mental autobiography comprising his minor contributions now republished, together with biographical and historical sketches of all his writings. New York, Putnams, 1913-1918, 6 vols.

Outlines of Sociology. New York, Macmillan, 1898, 301 pp.

The Psychic Factors of Civilization. Boston, Ginn, 1906, 369 pp.

Pure Sociology. New York, Macmillan, 1903, 607 pp.

WATSON, JOHN BROADUS (1878-   )

Psychology from the Standpoint of a Behaviorist. Philadelphia, Lippincott, 1919, 429 pp.

WEBB, SIDNEY (1859-   )

POTTER, BEATRICE (1858-   )

A Constitution for a Socialist Commonwealth of Great Britain. London, Longmans, 1920, 364 pp.

Industrial Democracy. London, Longmans, 1897, 2 vols. (rev. ed., 1911, 929 pp.)

The Decay of Capitalist Civilization. New York, Harcourt-Brace, 1923, 242 pp.

WESTERMARCK, EDWARD ALEXANDER (1862-   )

History of Human Marriage. New York, and London, Macmillan, 1894, 644 pp. (5th ed. 1921, 3 vols.).

WEYL, WALTER EDWARD (1873-1919)

The New Democracy: an essay on certain political and economic tendencies in the United States. New York, Macmillan, 1912, 370 pp.

Tired Radicals. New York, Huebsch, 1921, 223 pp.

WILLOUGHBY, WESTEL WOODBURY (1867-   )

An Examination of the Nature of the State; a study in political philosophy. New York, Macmillan, 1896, 448 pp.

WISSLER, CLARK (1870-   )

The American Indian: an introduction to the anthropology of the new world. New York, McMurtrie, 1917, 435 pp. (Oxford University Press, 2nd ed., 1922).

Man and Culture. New York, Crowell, 1923, 371 pp.

WITHERS, HARTLEY (1867-   )

The case for Capitalism. New York, Dutton, 1920, 255 pp.

WORMS, RÉNE (1869-   )

Organisme et société. Paris, Giard & Brière, 1896, 419 pp.

Philosophie des sciences sociales. Paris, Giard & Briére, 1904-1913, 3 vols.

WRIGHT, CARROLL DAVIDSON (1840–1909)

Outline of Practical Sociology: with special reference to American conditions. New York, Longmans, 1900, 431 pp.

WUNDT, WILHELM MAX (1832–1920)

Elements of Folk Psychology: outlines of a psychological history of the development of minkind. London, Unwin; New York, Macmillan, 1916, 532 pp. (Translated by Edward Leroy Schaub).

YERKES, ROBERT MEARNS (1876-   )

YOAKUM, CLARENCE STONE (1879–   )

The Army Mental Tests. New York, Holt, 1920 303 pp.

INDEX

Adams, John, economic factors in the state, 69
adaptation, a social process, Vaccaro on, 102, 171
administrative syndicalism, 41, 165–6
Althusius, Johannes, on group composition of state, 7, 11, 29–30
anthropologists, critical, or historical-analytical, school of, 49
  on the origins of the state, 49–52
  evolutionary school of, on the origins of the state, 46–9
Aristotle, on economic factors in the state, 68
Austin, John, 7, 12

Bachofen, Johann Jakob, on primitive society, 46
Bagehot, Walter, forms of the state, 95
  progress, 170–71
  social significance of discussion, 75
  stages of political development, 55
Baldwin, James Mark, community and society, 35
  individual and society, 198
  psychological factors in the state, 74, 76

Barker, Ernest, nature of state, 30
Beard, Charles Austin, economic factors in the state, 73n
  sociology and the state, 27
Belloc, Hilaire, criticism of state activity, 159
Bentham, Jeremy, 7, 75–6
Bentley, Arthur Fisher, classification of the state, 81–2
  criticism of doctrine of sovereignty, 127
  group pressures in the state, 103ff
  political party as an interest-group, 115–16
  separation of powers, 111
biological factors in the state, 57–64
biology, and democratic dogmas, 92
Boas, Franz, founder of critical and scientific anthropology, 49–52
  views on racial capacities, 60–1
Bodin, Jean, 11, 64
Brunhes, Jean, geographic factors in the state, 65, 66
Burgess, John William, lawyers and political life in the United States, 12
  sovereignty, 79

political theory, complexes of
  writers, 214–15
  psychoanalysis and, 214–15
  relation of to social environment, 9–10, 209ff
Polybius, origins of the state,
  53
population problems, and state,
  57ff
Pound, Roscoe, sociological
  jurisprudence, 6, 12
powers, governmental, separation of, 111–12
processes of government, 100ff
progress, sociological theories
  of, 168ff
propaganda and public opinion,
  202, 203–4
"protocracy," Giddings' on,
  120–21
psychoanalysis and political
  theory, 214–15
psychological classes in the
  state, 62
psychological factors in politics, 73–76
public opinion, Lippmann's
  analysis of, 202–4
  pluralistic or monistic, 204–5
  sociological analysis of, 200–6

Quetelet, Adolphe, founder of
  social statistics, 59

racial superiority, theories of,
  59–61
Ratzel, Friedrich, geography
  and the state, 65
Ratzenhofer, Gustav, forms of
  state, 95–6
  group basis of state, 102
  group interests, 116–17

nature of state, 32–4
progress, 171
stages of political development, 55–6
Reclus, Elisee, geographic factors in the state, 65
representation of interests,
  107–9
representative government, sociological theories of, 105ff
  territorial basis, critique of,
  106–9
revolution, sociological theory
  of, 179–80
Ricardian Socialists, on economic factors in the state,
  11, 70
rights of man, 6, 146ff
rights, political, sociological
  views on, 146ff
Ripley, William Zebina, Aryan
  race, 60
Ritter, Karl, founder of anthropogeography, 64–5
Robinson, James Harvey, anachronistic and futile nature
  of modern education, 207
Ross, Edward Alsworth, attitude towards social progress, 173
  forms of the state, 97–8
  immigration as a social process, 190
  psychological factors in the
  state, 74
  Russian revolution, 180
  social control, 137–9, 196
  sociological theory of sovereignty, 137–9
  theory of state activity, 165
Rousseau, Jean Jacques, representative government, 106
Russia, sociology in, 22